Cycles of Knowing and Growing

Principal Author
Barbara Ann Novelli

Contributing Authors

Barbara Battcher
Maribeth Clark
Carol Gossett
Suzy Gazlay

Wendy Knight
Judy Kirk
Nicki Klevan
Marilyn McMasters

Illustrators
Margie Anderson
Margo Pocock
Brenda Richmond

Editor
Betty Cordel

Desktop Publisher
Kristy Shuler

This book contains materials developed by the AIMS Education Foundation. **AIMS** (**A**ctivities **I**ntegrating **M**athematics and **S**cience) began in 1981 with a grant from the National Science Foundation. The non-profit AIMS Education Foundation publishes hands-on instructional materials (books and the monthly *AIMS* magazine) that integrate curricular disciplines such as mathematics, science, language arts, and social studies. The Foundation sponsors a national program of professional development through which educators may gain both an understanding of the AIMS philosophy and expertise in teaching by integrated, hands-on methods.

ISBN **1-881431-65-7**

Printed in the United States of America

I Hear and I Forget

I See and I Remember

I Do and I Understand

—Chinese Proverb

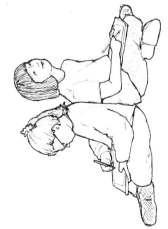

Cycles of Knowing and Growing
Table of Contents

Cycles of Knowing and Growing

Introduction

Mary Baratta-Lorton in the book *Mathematics Their Way* (Addison-Wesley. Reading, MA. 1976.) says, "Looking for patterns trains the mind to search out and discover the similarities that bind seemingly unrelated information together in a whole. … A child who expects things to 'make sense' looks for the sense in things and from this sense develops understanding. A child who does not see patterns often does not expect things to make sense and sees all events as discrete, separate, and unrelated." *Cycles of Knowing and Growing* is based on the overarching theme of science, *patterns of change.* Cycles and trends are two types of patterns explored in this book.

At an early age children begin to ask questions and observe patterns in their world. What child doesn't notice the repeatable pattern of day and night? What child isn't intrigued by a pile of fallen leaves? What child hasn't stopped to look at a flower that bloomed from a bud they noticed the day before? What child hasn't boasted about how big he/she has gotten?

Children are observers of patterns, but frequently they have not been provided the opportunity to analyze them or to view them as parts to whole. This book, *Cycles of Knowing and Growing*, offers young learners the opportunity to attend to real-world patterns as they emerge over time.

As children become familiar with their world, they can be guided to observe changes, including cyclical changes like night and day, the phases of the moon, and the seasons. They can look at the changes in themselves or other animals such as caterpillars. Given enough experience and focused observation, they can make predictions about what will happen next. By focusing on a natural object such as a tree and observing it over time, children start to make generalizations about changes in other natural objects. Experiences for young children should concentrate on observations, descriptions, and the finding of patterns. Given these beginning experiences children will later be able to make more sophisticated observations and predictions in relation to change. In later years they will be able to make explanations and applications which are based on those previous experiences and observations. *Benchmarks for Science Literacy* (American Association for the Advancement of Science, p. 272) recommends that "Children should attend to change and describe it. Only after they have a storehouse of experience with change of different kinds are they ready to start thinking about patterns of change in the abstract."

Cycles of Knowing and Growing is optimistically based on the hope that teachers between Kindergarten and third grade will share in providing children with opportunities to analyze these natural cycles and trends over several years. It makes sense that the seed from the pumpkin grown in "Just A Little Sprout" be the same seeds planted the following year in grade one, two, or three. It also makes sense that the pumpkins grown from the year before, be the pumpkins observed in "Golden House." Students that have observed the moon in first grade can continue their "Moon Watchers Journal" in second and even third grade.

We hope that *Cycles of Knowing and Growing* will provide primary teachers a forum of sharing and collaboration so that children will become pattern seekers for the rest of their lives.

Project 2061 Benchmarks for Science Literacy*

AIMS is committed to remaining at the cutting edge of providing curriculum materials that are user-friendly, educationally sound, developmentally appropriate and aligned with the recommendations found in national education reform documents.

The Nature of Science

- People can often learn about things around them by just observing those things carefully, but sometimes they can learn more by doing something to the things and noting what happens.

- Tools such as thermometers, magnifiers, rulers, or balances often give more information about things than can be obtained by just observing things without their help.

- Describing things as accurately as possible is important in science because it enables people to compare their observations with those of others.

- A lot can be learned about plants and animals by observing them closely, but care must be taken to know the needs of living things and how to provide for them in the classroom.

The Physical Setting

- The sun can be seen only in the daytime, but the moon can be seen sometimes at night and sometimes during the day. The sun, moon and stars all appear to move slowly across the sky.

- The moon looks a little different every day, but looks the same again about every four weeks.

- Like all planets and stars, the earth is approximately spherical in shape. The rotation of the earth on its axis every 24 hours produces the night-and-day cycle. To people on earth, this turning of the planet makes it seem as though the sun, moon, planets, and stars are orbiting the earth once a day.

- Some events in nature have a repeating pattern. The weather changes some from day to day, but things such as temperature and rain (or snow) tend to be high, low, or medium in the same months every year.

- Change is something that happens to many things.

- Animals and plants sometimes cause changes in their surroundings.

- Things can be done to materials to change some of their properties, but not all materials respond the same way to what is done to them.

The Living Environment

- Some animals and plants are alike in the way they look and things they do, and others are very different from one another.

- There is variation among individuals of one kind within a population.

- Most living things need water, food, and air.

- Animals eat plants or other animals for food and may also use plants (or even other animals) for shelter and nesting.

- Many materials can be recycled and used again, sometimes in different forms.

The Designed World	• Some kinds of materials are better than others for making any particular thing. Materials that are better in some ways (such as stronger or cheaper) may be worse in other ways (heavier or harder to cut).	• Several steps are usually involved in making things. • Some materials can be used over again.
The Mathematical World	• Simple graphs can help to tell about observations. • Some things are more likely to happen than others. Some events can be predicted well and some cannot. Sometimes	people aren't sure what will happen because they don't know everything that might be having an effect.
Common Themes	• People can keep track of some things, seeing where they come from and where they go.	• Some changes are so slow or so fast they are hard to see.
Habits of Mind	• Keep records of their investigations and observations and not change the records later.	

* American Association for the Advancement of Science. *Benchmarks for Science Literacy.* Oxford University Press. New York. 1993.

National Science Education Standards*

Abilities Necessary to do Scientific Inquiry	• Employ simple equipment and tools to gather data and extend the senses.
Understandings About Scientific Inquiry	• Scientists use different kinds of investigations depending on the questions they are trying to answer. Types of investigations include describing objects, events, and organisms; classifying them; and doing a fair test (experimenting). • Simple instruments, such as magnifiers, thermometers, and rulers, provide more information than scientists obtain using only their senses.
Properties of Objects and Materials	• Objects have many observable properties, including size, weight, shape, color, temperature, and the ability to react with other substances. Those properties can be measured using tools, such as rulers, balances, and thermometers.
Position and Motion of Objects	• The position of an object can be described by locating it relative to another object or the background. • An object's motion can be described by tracing and measuring its position over time.
Life Cycles of Organisms	• Plants and animals have life cycles that include being born, developing into adults, reproducing, and eventually dying. The details of this life cycle are different for different organisms.
Organisms and Their Environment	• All organisms cause changes in the environment where they live. Some of these changes are detrimental to the organism or other organisms, whereas others are beneficial.
Properties of Earth Materials	• Earth materials are solid rocks and soils, water and the gases of the atmosphere. The varied materials have different physical and chemical properties, which make them useful in different ways, for example, as building materials, as sources of fuel, or for growing the plants we use as food. Earth materials provide many of the resources that humans use. • Soils have properties of color and texture, capacity to retain water, and ability to support the growth of many kinds of plants, including those in our food supply.
Objects in the Sky	• The sun, moon, stars, clouds, birds, and airplanes all have properties, locations, and movements that can be observed and described.
Changes in the Earth and Sky	• Objects in the sky have patterns of movement. The sun, for example, appears to move across the sky in the same way every day, but its path changes slowly over the seasons. The moon moves across the sky on a daily basis much like the sun. The observable shape of the moon changes from day to day in a cycle that lasts about a month.
Types of Resources	• The supply of many resources are limited. If used, resources can be extended through recycling and decreased use.

* National Research Council. *National Science Education Standards*. National Academy Press. Washington, D.C. 1996.

Curriculum and Evaluation Standards for School Mathematics*

Mathematics as Communication	• Relate physical materials, pictures and diagrams to mathematical ideas
Mathematical Connections	• Use mathematics in other curriculum areas
Estimation	• Apply estimation when working with quantities, measurement, computation and problem solving
Number Sense and Numeration	• Construct number meanings through real-world experiences and the use of physical materials • Understand our numeration system by relating counting, grouping, and place-value concepts
Geometry and Spatial Sense	• Investigate and predict the results of combining, subdividing, and changing shapes • Develop spatial sense • Recognize and appreciate geometry in their world
Measurement	• Understand the attributes of length, capacity, weight, mass, area, volume, time, temperature and angle • Develop the process of measuring and concepts related to units of measurement • Make and use measurements in problem and everyday situations
Statistics and Probability	• Collect, organize and describe data • Construct, read and interpret displays of data • Formulate and solve problems that involve collecting and analyzing data
Patterns and Relationships	• Recognize, describe, extend and create a variety of patterns

*National Council of Teachers of Mathematics. *Curriculum and Evaluation Standards for School Mathematics*. NCTM. Reston, VA. 1989.

Look At Me Now!

Topic
Growth and development

Key Questions
1. How have we changed since we were born?
2. How will we change this year?

Focus
Young learners will investigate changes in their growth.

Guiding Document
Project 2061 Benchmarks
- *Change is something that happens to many things.*
- *Tools such as thermometers, magnifiers, rulers, or balances often give more information about things than can be obtained by just observing things without their help.*
- *Some animals and plants are alike in the way they look and things they do, and others are very different from one another.*
- *There is variation among individuals of one kind within a population.*

NRC Standard
- *Plants and animals have life cycles that include being born, developing into adults, reproducing, and eventually dying. The details of this life cycle are different for different organisms.*

NCTM Standards
- *Develop the process of measuring and concepts related to units of measurement*
- *Make and use measurements in problem and everyday situations*

Math
Measuring

Science
Life science
  growth and development

Integrated Processes
Observing
Estimating
Predicting
Comparing and contrasting
Communicating

Materials
For each student:
  1 meter string
  2 meters of string of a different color
  gallon-size zipper-type plastic bag
  parent letter
  12" X 18" drawing paper

For the class:
  metric tapes

For the teacher:
  a baby picture

Background Information
Change and patterns of change are themes that are imbedded in many science frameworks. One type of pattern of change is the change that occurs in trends. Growth is such a pattern. In most cases, students will see that over time, they grow taller.

In this activity, students will use lengths of string to represent their current heights and their birth lengths. They will make comparisons of their results to others in the classroom. This measurement component of the activity is continued throughout the year with students observing their growth and comparing to previous results. To add interest, they will share stories about their infancy and baby pictures and other artifacts, if available.

Management
1. It is important that as many children as possible bring birth lengths, hand and foot prints, and pictures to school for this project. It may be necessary to make additional home contacts and wait a few days before continuing this activity to enable more students to bring in pictures and needed information.
2. Find a display area in which to post the growth charts so students can continue to compare their growth over time. If this place is not available, store the growth charts by punching a hole in the top of each and hooking them together with a looseleaf book ring or shower curtain hook.
3. Copy the parent letter and insert one into each large zipper-type plastic bag to allow safe travel to and from school for pictures, measurement information, and artifacts.
4. Set up a large bulletin board for display of children's pictures and artifacts by dividing it into grids with yarn. Provide each child with a grid space of approximately 15 cm X 15 cm. Students can label the grids with their names. Other items can be added as they are shared.

5. Children who are not able to bring photos or artifacts may draw a picture of themselves as a baby or cut out magazine pictures of how they might have looked as a baby. If they cannot provide information about birth lengths, give them an average birth length to use. (One source reports that the average length at birth for a child in the United States is between 20 and 21 inches.)

6. Before the measurement session begins, the sunflowers should be cut out and colored, and the stems copied on colored paper. Students will need to print their names on their own sunflowers. The teacher can place the poem above the growth charts.

Procedure

Prior to the measurement activity:

1. Ask students to tell stories about when they were babies. Allow several students time to share.

2. Show them your own baby picture and ask how you've changed since that picture was taken.

3. Explain to the class that some homework is necessary before the class can do the activity *Look At Me Now!* Tell students they are to take the letter home to their parents and help their parents collect the pictures and other information needed to determine how they have changed since they were born?

4. Once children have brought in the needed information, allow them time to share their baby pictures with the class and talk about how they have changed. After they share their pictures and baby artifacts, have students put them in their grids on the bulletin board.

Measurement:

5. Help students cut string the same length as their birth lengths. (Young learners do not need to understand units of measurement at this time, they should instead focus on the idea that the length of string represents their birth length.)

6. Allow time for students to explore and compare their own birth length with their classmate's birth length. Students will often place their birth lengths side-by-side to compare, but if they do not, encourage them with questions that prompt this type of comparison.

7. Ask students to find as many things as possible in the room as long as their birth length. On a blank piece of drawing paper, have students sketch or use inventive spelling to write things they found that were the same length. Encourage them to compare their birth length with the current height (see *Discussion*).

8. Give students a different colored string. Cut it to their current height. Allow time for them to compare and share their comparisons (growth since birth, tallest student has longest string, etc).

9. Have the students take their two measurement strings to their sunflower growth chart and tape them to the chart. They may need adult assistance. After attaching the strings, label them with a leaf from the student page that has been dated.

10. The measurement segment of this activity should be repeated at least one more time in the year. Each time the string should be attached to the growth chart after extensive comparison.

Discussion

1. How many baby lengths does it take to equal your current height? How do you know?

2. By looking at how much you have grown since you were a baby, how much do you think you will grow by January? ... next summer?

3. How does your baby length compare to others in the class?

4. What are some other ways that you have changed?

Extensions

1. Invite parents to bring in newborn babies. A class could "adopt" a baby and have the parent bring it in several times during the year so they can measure its growth.

2. Have students make a Unifix cube train equal to their birth length. They should then bring these to a rug area and place them side-by-side. Ask students what they observe about the class birth lengths. If they take off Unifix cubes from the longer trains and add them to the shorter, the students will come up with an average birth length for the class. Repeat this for current height. Comparisons can be made between average lengths and their personal lengths.

3. Students can use the hand prints brought in to compare their current hand prints. How many baby hand prints does your current height equal? Do the same with their foot prints.

4. Have students compare themselves to a tree or sunflower and keep track of their growth in relation to the growth of the plant.

Curriculum Correlation

Literature

Allen, Marjorie N. and Shelley Rotner. *Changes.* Macmillan Publishing Co. New York. 1991.

Home Link

Parents can make a growth chart at home to keep track of their own child's growth.

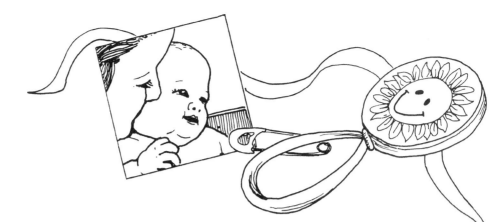

Dear Families,

   In school, we are learning about how we grow and change. Would you please help us? Can you help us find our baby pictures so they can be shared with the class? If there are other things that might help us learn about how we have grown and changed (baby foot and hand prints, baby clothes, etc.), we would like to see them, too. Please put the pictures and other items in the plastic bag so we can carefully take them to school and then back home.

   Please also give us the following information:

My length at birth was _____ .

                    Thank you,

Child's name _____

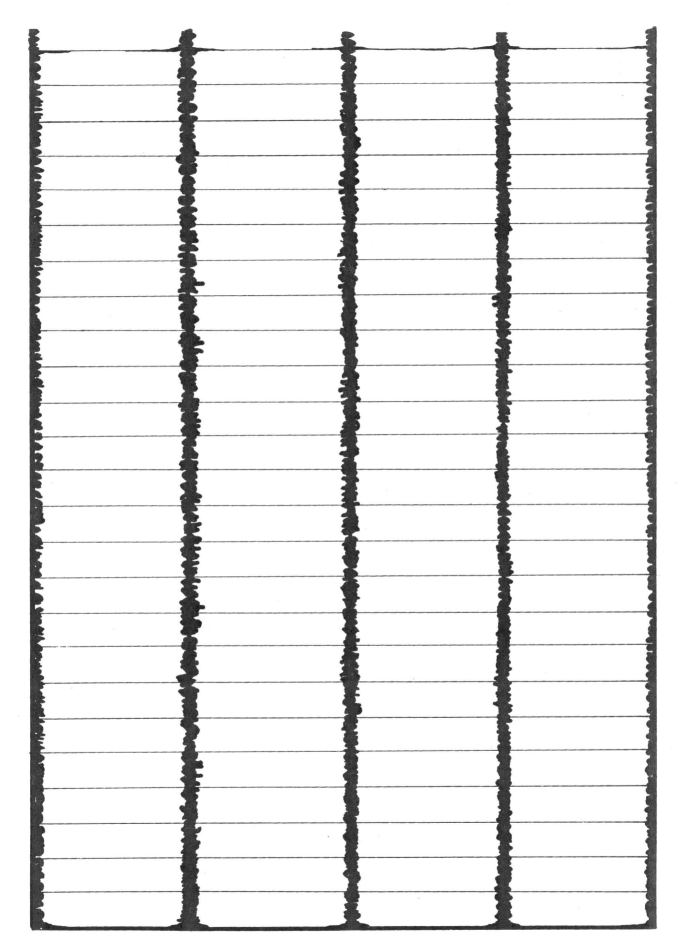

Look At Me !

Look at me,
See how high!
Up, up, up, I'm growing.
Look at me!
Look real close!
Don't you think it's showing?

Barbara Ann Novelli

I AM GROWING

Words by Suzy Gazlay   Tune: Are You Sleeping?

I am grow-ing, I am grow-ing.

Look at me! Look at me!

I am get-ting big - ger,

I am get-ting big - ger.

You can see, you can see.

As a baby, as a baby,
I was small, I was small.
Now I am a big kid, now I am a big kid;
I am tall, I am tall.

I'll keep growing, I'll keep growing;
So will you, so will you.
We'll be even taller, we'll be even taller
When we're through, when we're through.

Tell Me When Your Birthday Comes

Topic
Developing an awareness of the passing of time between birthdays

Key Question
How many times has the yearly cycle of months been completed since you were born?

Focus
Students will sit in a circle corresponding to their month of birth. Each time the yearly cycle of months is chanted, students will discuss the change in their age corresponding to the passing of time.

Guiding Documents
Project 2061 Benchmarks
- *Change is something that happens to many things.*
- *Some changes are so slow or so fast they are hard to see.*
- *Some things are more likely to happen than others. Some events can be predicted well and some cannot. Sometimes people aren't sure what will happen because they don't know everything that might be having an effect.*

NCTM Standards
- *Recognize, describe, extend, and create a variety of patterns*
- *Construct, read, and interpret displays of data*

Math
Time
    months
    years
Counting

Science
Life science
    change
    growth

Integrated Processes
Observing
Contrasting and Comparing
Communicating
Collecting and recording data
Applying

Materials
For the class:
    month labels (provided)
    yarn
    magazine pictures of children of ages birth through six or seven
    birthday cake chart

For each student:
    birthday cake tab book
    crown
    set of 3/4" dots (see *Management*)

Background Information
The very day after their birthday, young children will often ask when their next birthday will come. They have not developed a sense of this relatively large scale time frame. This activity will focus on the yearly cycle of months corresponding to their birthdays. While it is evident that the students will still not truly understand the passing of time, they will, however, begin to develop an awareness of the passing of months before their next birthday.

To help develop a sense of personal history, students will share what they remember about being one, two, or three. They will be encouraged to remember details of their childhood. Parents can help them by reflecting on memories of them at younger ages.

Management
1. Ask families to send in a picture of their child at each of their various ages. Before sending in these pictures, encourage the families to label, discuss, and share memories of the child at each age.
2. Look through magazines or study prints to find pictures which represent the developmental stages and ages of the students in the class.
3. The number of pages in the birthday book and the number of dots on the birthday crown will depend upon the age range of your students.
4. Select an area large enough for the students to sit in a circle which has been partitioned with thick yarn into 12 sections. The students will line up behind the label of the month of their birth.
5. Prepare a large birthday cake chart to record their thoughts about how they have changed over time.
6. Make the month labels using the graphics provided or use your own calendar labels.

Procedure

Part 1

1. Read *Changes* by Marjorie Allen and Shelly Rotner and discuss how all things change. Ask the children how they have changed over the months and years. List these things on a large birthday cake chart.

2. Direct students to make their birthday books by cutting along the broken lines. Have them stack the pages in order from the page with one candle on top to the page with eight candles on the bottom. Staple along the bottom edge of the book.

3. Discuss the months as they relate to class birthdays. Place the month labels on the floor in a circle as you chant the months. Ask students to indicate their birthday by standing behind their birthday month label. Direct the students to sit down in a line behind the month labels.

4. Ask them to tell you about their circle graph. (Make interpretations such as: more people in our class were born in April, nobody was born in September. There is the same number of people born in October and December.)

5. After this discussion of birth months, ask the students the *Key Question*. Clarify this question by asking how many times has it been October (or any other month) since they were born?

6. Teach the class the chant
   Winter, Spring, Summer, Fall,
   Months go by as I grow tall.
   January, February, March, April,
   May, June, July, August,
   September, October, November, December....
   Chant it over and over.

7. Ask them when they were born. Talk about what they looked like and acted like at birth (so they have been told.) If students have brought pictures, let them share their birth pictures at this time.

8. Tell them that you will walk slowly around the circle as they chant the months. When you come to January, ask those students who were born in January how old they would be when they experienced another January. [one-year old]

Have them bend the other pages back in their birthday book so only one candle shows. Students may bring up the fact that if they were born in May they are not quite one yet. Tell them that as you walk past them, they will become another year older. Discuss what they might have looked like and acted like when they were one. What things might they be able to do. Again, share pictures, theirs or the magazine pictures, to help them visualize a one-year old.

9. Walk around the circle as they slowly chant while holding up their cake book with one candle.

10. When returning to January, repeat the discussion about characteristics of a two-year old. Then repeat the chant, and walk around the circle while they hold two candles up in their book.

11. Continue this until you have arrived at everyone's age.

Part 2

(For ease of writing the procedure for this part, January is used as the example of the birth month. Students should be made to realize that their year will start with their own birthday month. Every time the teacher passes their birthday month, they will add a dot to their crowns.)

1. Read *Over and Over* by Charlotte Zolotow.

2. Have students cut out and assemble their crowns. Allow time for them to decorate their crowns. Direct them to not color the flames because they will put dots on these flames to represent their ages.

3. Have students wear their crowns and form the circle in which they again stand behind the month label of their birth. (Older students can also arrange themselves into order of the date of their birthday as well as the month.)

4. Repeat the chant several times, and then ask the *Key Question*. Distribute a strip of dots to each student. (The number of dots should correspond to the age span of the group).

5. Walk around the circle as the group chants the month poem. Tell the students that every time you walk in front of them, they will count another year. Again, discuss what they looked like at one, two, etc. They may have additional stories to tell or they may wish to share what their parents recorded or they drew in their birthday book.

6. Tell the students that they will begin to add a dot to their crowns when you pass by them this time. Repeat the procedure, adding a dot to the crown with each time you pass the students' birth months.

Discussion

1. How many more yearly cycles of months will be completed before you are ten?... twenty?

2. What are some ways most students in the class have changed?
3. What are some ways only a few in the class have changed? [hair color, eye color]
4. So far, which was your favorite birthday? Why?
5. How would you describe your birthday month?
6. What is the weather usually like on your birthday?
7. Why is it important to know the cycle of the months? When do you use it?

Extensions

1. Use the birthday book to do math equations. For example: four candles plus three candles can be writtten $4 + 3 = 7$; or eight candles up, fold two candles down and write $8 - 2 = 6$)
2. Touch the months on the band of the crown as class chants the months of the year.
3. Make a class book depicting the months of the year.
4. Keep your own records of what happens during each month you are in school.
5. At the end of the activity, move the month labels into a row on the floor and have the class make a real bar graph by placing their crowns above the appropriate month. Have the students go back to their seats. Use the graph sheet to make a representational graph of the birthdays in class by coloring a crown for each birthday in the corresponding month.

Curriculum Correlation

Allen, Marjorie. N., Rotner. *Changes*. Macmillan. New York. 1991.

Ichikawa, Satomi. *Happy Birthday, A Book of Birthday Celebrations*. Philomel Books. New York. 1987.

Johnston. Tony, *Yonder*. Dial Books. New York. 1988.

Zolotow, Charlotte. *Over and Over*. HarperCollins Publishers. New York. 1957.

Home Link

Students should take their birthday books home and share them with their families. The families should be encouraged to add stories to each page and send them back to share with the class. Students should be encouraged to teach their families the chant.

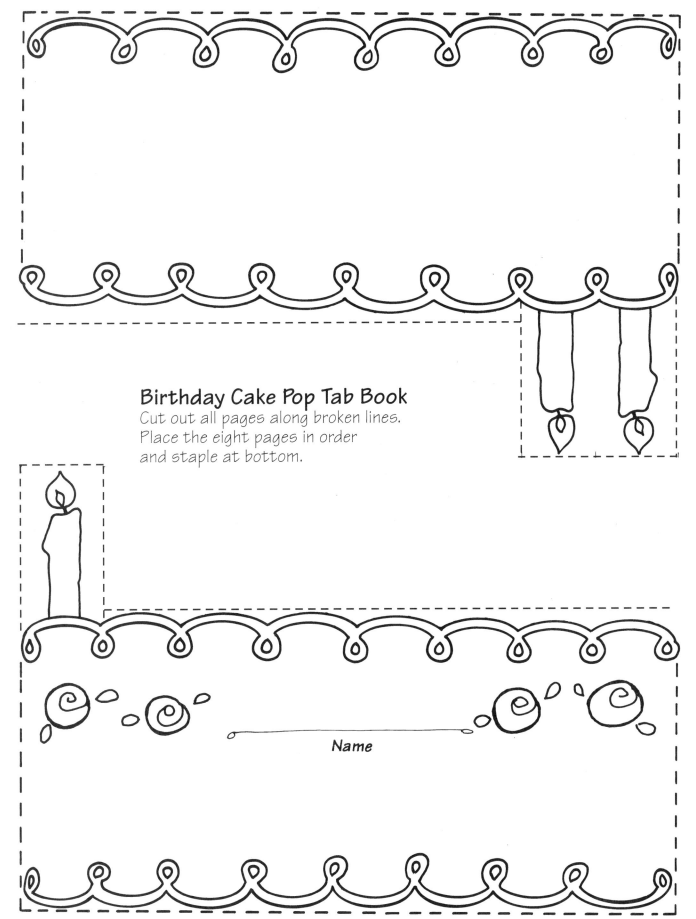

Birthday Cake Pop Tab Book
Cut out all pages along broken lines.
Place the eight pages in order
and staple at bottom.

Name

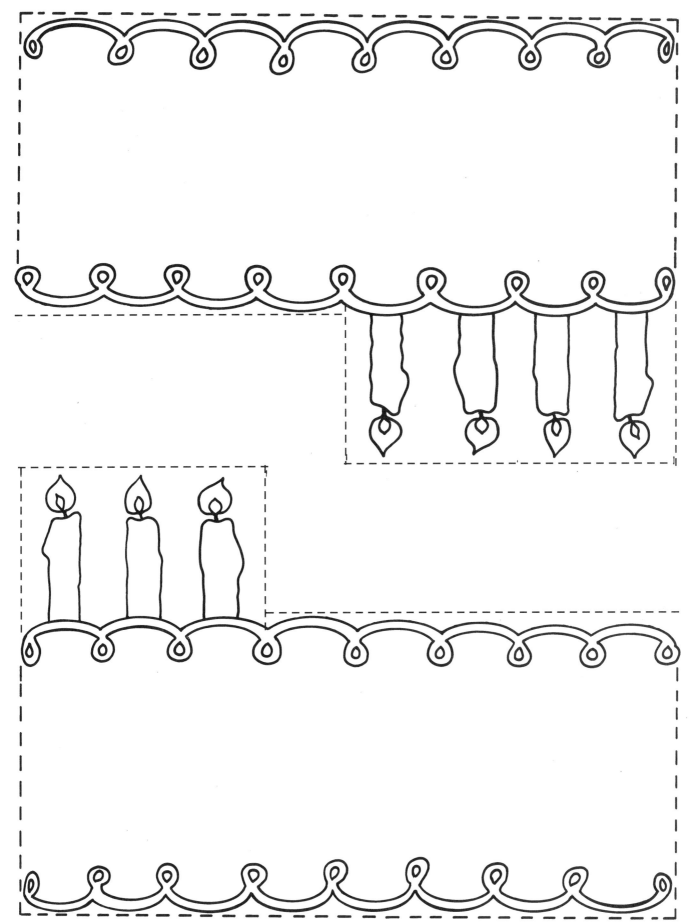

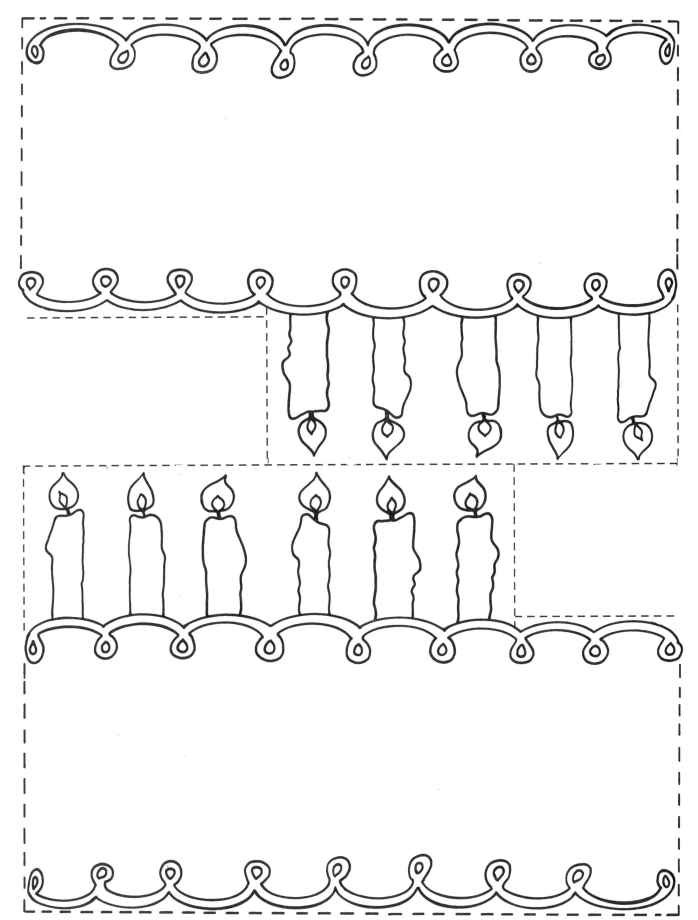

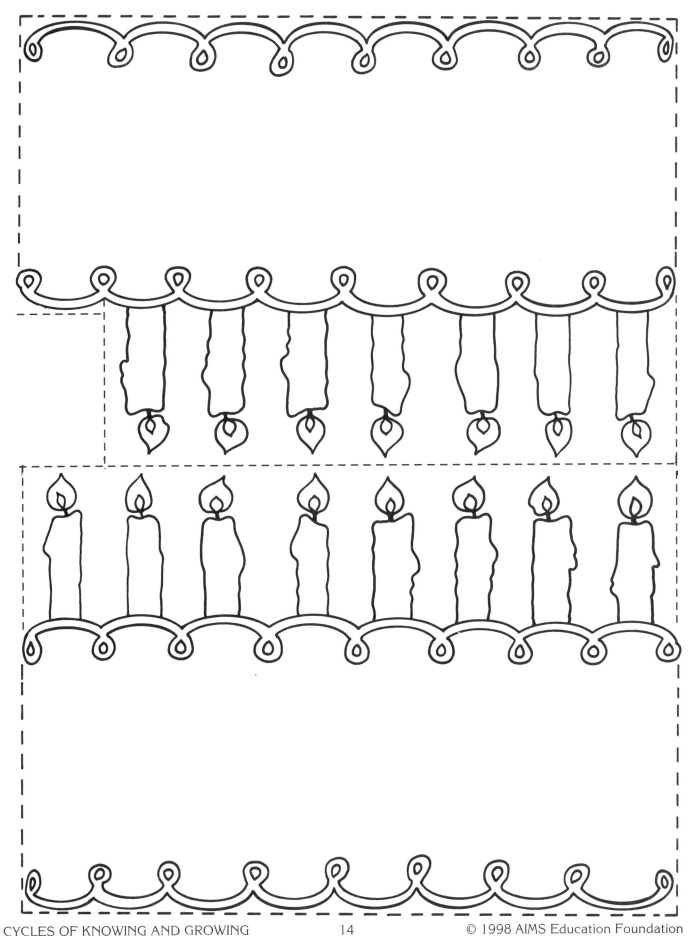

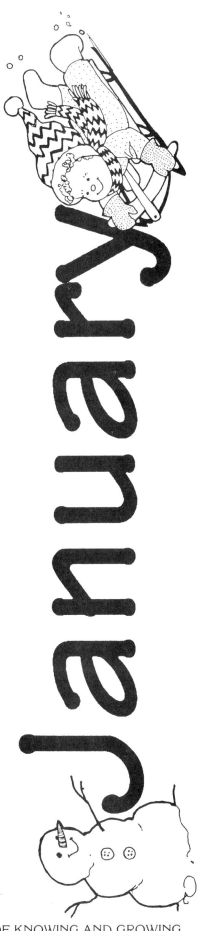

January

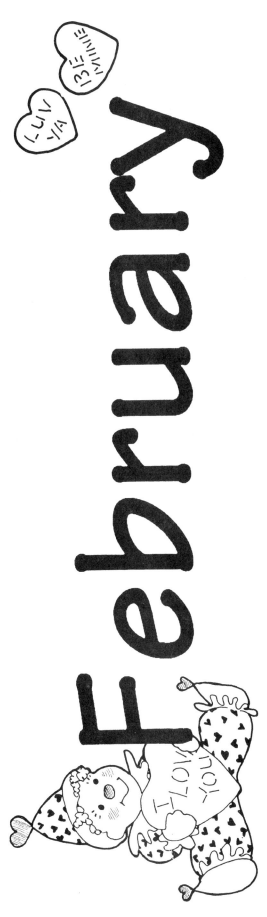

February

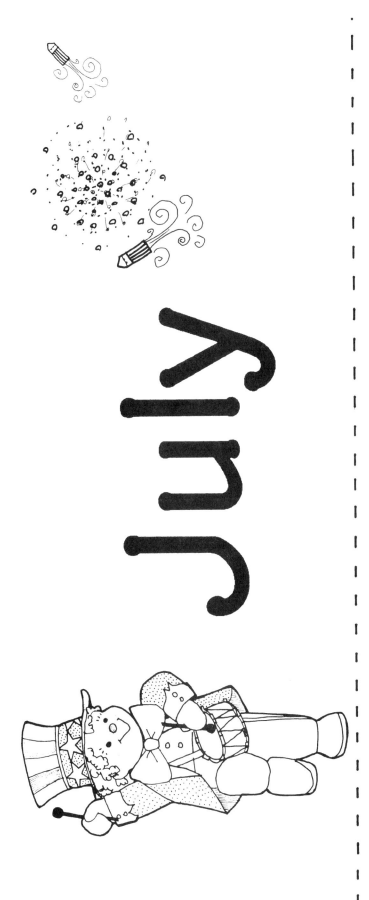

July

August

September

October

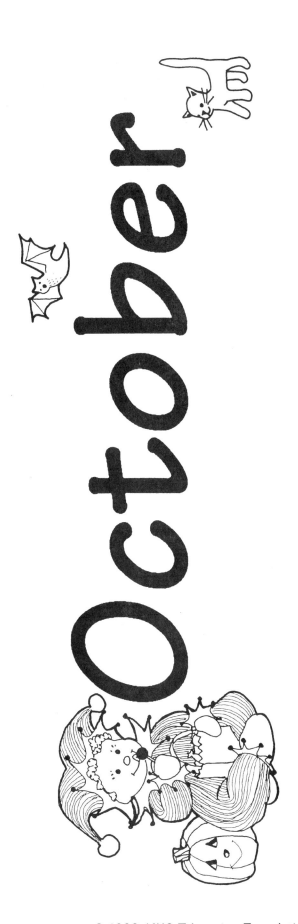

November

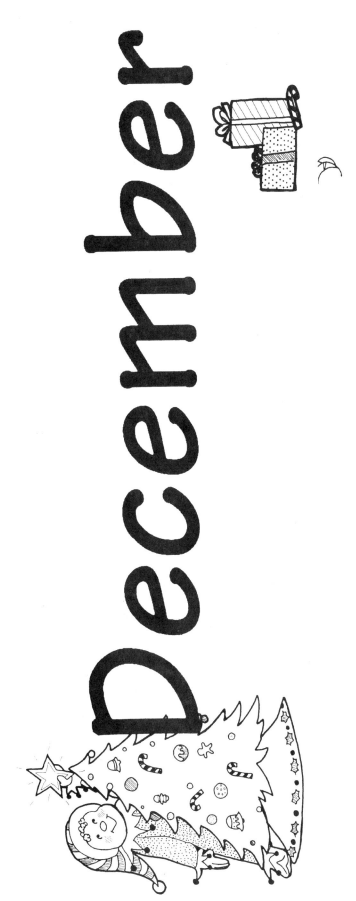

December

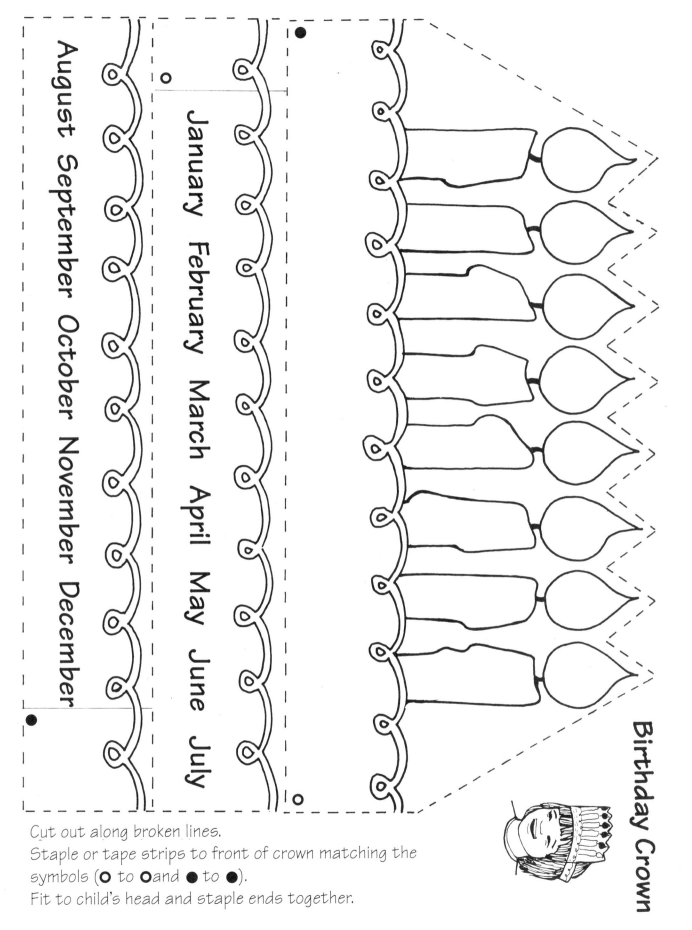

August September October November December

January February March April May June July

Cut out along broken lines.
Staple or tape strips to front of crown matching the symbols (O to O and ● to ●).
Fit to child's head and staple ends together.

Birthday Crown

Birthda

Jan.	Feb.	March	April	May	June

y Graph

July	Aug.	Sept.	Oct.	Nov.	Dec.

A Time of Their Own

Topic
Life cycles of moths and butterflies

Key Question
How do butterflies and moths change as they go through their life cycle?

Focus
The class will observe and compare the metamorphoses of butterflies and moths.

Guiding Documents
Project 2061 Benchmarks
- *A lot can be learned about plants and animals by observing them closely, but care must be taken to know the needs of living things and how to provide for them in the classroom.*
- *Some animals and plants are alike in the way they look and in the things they do, and others are very different from one another.*
- *Change is something that happens to many things.*

NCR Standard
- *Plants and animals have life cycles that include being born, developing into adults, reproducing and eventually dying. The details of this life cycle are different for different organisms.*

NCTM Standards
- *Understand the attributes of length, capacity, weight, mass, area, volume, time, temperature, and angle.*
- *Make and use measurements in problems and everyday situations*
- *Recognize, describe, extend, and create a variety of patterns*

Math
Measuring
time
area

Science
Life science
life cycles
change

Integrated Processes
Observing
Comparing and contrasting
Communicating

Materials
For each group:
2 or 3 larvae of butterflies or moths
additional food for the larva
transparent container for food and larvae
17 sheets construction paper (12" x 18"), or large chart paper
one-centimeter grid paper
markers
water colors
20 strips each of three colors of construction paper, 1" x 9"
hand lens, optional

Sources for Larva:
Insect Lore, 132 Beech St., Shafter, CA 93263. Telephone: 1-800-LIVE BUG

NASCO Scientific, 901 Janesville Ave., Fort Atkinson, WI 53538-0901. Telephone: 1-414-563-2446

NASCO WEST, 1524 Princeton Ave., Modesto, CA 95352-3837. Telephone: 1-209-529-6957

Background Information
While butterflies and moths are somewhat different in appearance, their metamorphoses are very similar. Both butterflies and moths go through a *complete metamorphosis* which means they change from egg, to larva, to pupa, to adult.

Both moth and butterfly *eggs* vary in color and size, although all are usually two millimeters or smaller. In the *larval* stage, the caterpillars are very diverse looking. Some caterpillars eat very specific food, while others eat a variety. The *pupal* stage is somewhat different in the two. The larva of a butterfly attaches its tail to a food plant and then the skin splits and is wriggled off revealing the chrysalis. The moth wraps itself in a silk coat. The chrysalis is inside this outer covering. Most moths remain in the pupal stage longer than butterflies. Some remain in this stage for many months, while most butterflies stay in the pupal stage for only a few weeks. When the *adult* butterflies or moths emerge, they look somewhat different. The moths usually have a thicker, "fuzzier" body. Their antennae are thicker and more feathery-like than the butterflies' longer and thinner ones.

Butterflies and moths provide an excellent glimpse of one of the most wondrous processes in nature, the metamorphosis of an insect. Both are dazzling performers in the air and hold the fascination of children and adults.

Management

1. The teacher should find a source for butterfly or moth larvae (caterpillars). Many larval forms can be found locally. If you catch the insect in larval form, collect a large amount of its food source at the same time and keep it in water or the refrigerator. Ask an entomology group, the local fish and game department, or a pest control agency for advice on where to search. The larva may also be ordered from supply houses. We have included supply houses which sell the larval form of butterflies and moths. If ordering larvae, make certain they can survive when released in your area. Also check to make sure you are not introducing a species that will do harm in your area.

2. If possible, use both butterflies and moths so that students can compare and contrast their stages.

3. Check reference books to determine the length of time the butterfly or moth remains in the pupal stage. Some moths will stay in the cocoon for months. Student interest remains higher if the moth chosen for observation has a pupal stage of less than a month.

4. Students will work in groups of four observing their butterfly chrysalis or moth cocoon.

5. Collect clear containers which allow every member of the group to observe daily changes.

6. Set aside time each day for observations and class reports.

7. When handling any live creature, it is important to handle them with respect and care. A class discussion focusing on the care of all living things should be scheduled before handing out the larval form. A class chart can be developed to state the rules for handling and caring for living things.

8. This activity has several different facets:
   - A group big book is constructed during the observations.
   - The group accounts for the amount of time for both the larval and pupal stages by making a paper chain for each day in that stage.
   - The students will use grid paper to determine the amount of food eaten by the larvae.
   - A student's journal could also be used during the activity.
   - As a culmination, the students make a film strip and write a script to describe the metamorphosis of the butterfly or moth. This can serve as an assessment of the activity.

9. Since the big book is a continuing process, it is best if art supplies are available at all times. This will allow groups to illustrate a new page in their big book when they observe something interesting.

(Following you will find an open-ended approach for use by students who are prepared for more independence in their investigations.)

> *Open-ended:* Students may observe the metamorphosis of their moth or butterfly and decide a way to report the changes to a group. The teacher may wish to use part of the blacklines or none at all to make it a totally original work.

Procedure

1. Allow students time to observe the larval form of their butterfly or moth. Encourage them to use hand lenses for more careful observation. To make page one of the group's big book, direct members to work together to use art supplies and a large sheet of construction paper or chart paper to illustrate the larvae. Urge them also to write about their observations. After completing this, have students display their pages and share what they observed.

2. Ask the *Key Question* and allow time for class discussion. Have students make predictions of what the next stage will be. Inform them that they will make daily observations of the larvae, keeping a record of these in their math/science journal. Then every two or three days they will make a new page for their big book and report the changes to the class.

3. Have each group make a paper chain for the first day and attach it to the *Larva stage* label. For each day the caterpillar stays in the larval stage, the students should add a link of the same color to the paper chain.

4. Before putting the larva and food in the observation container, have group members trace around one leaf on one-centimeter grid paper. This will remind them of the size of the leaf before the caterpillar begins eating. After the larva has eaten some of the leaf, direct students to place the eaten leaf on the grid paper, trace around the holes, and color in the parts eaten. Encourage them to continue to record the amount of food (leaf) the larva has eaten and to record these observations in the big books as well as journal writings.

5. When the larva spins the cocoon or forms a chrysalis, direct the groups to add another page to their big book and report their findings to the class. Have them also record the actual form of this stage in their math/science journals. Have them continue observing the daily changes and every two or three days make another page for the groups' big books.

6. Ask the students how long they think the pupal (cocoon or chrysalis) stage will last? Have the class share their predictions and then each group should make a paper link of a different color to represent the first day in this *Pupa stage*. They will continue to keep track of the days by adding a same-color link each day until the butterfly or moth emerges.

7. Have students predict what will emerge from the cocoon or chrysalis. Have them record their predictions in their journals.

8. When the butterfly or moth emerges, have students take a walking field trip within the classroom to observe and discuss each groups' critters. When students return to their desks, allow them time to compare and contrast what they observed, add another page in their big book, and share their findings and illustrations from the big books.

9. Discuss what will happen after the adult stage. Since the egg stage is not easily observed, show them pictures, film strips, or a video that depicts this stage.

10. If you have found the larva locally, it is best to release the butterfly or moth at this time and discuss the next phase with the students. If you have purchased your butterfly or moth kit through a supplier, check the directions in the kit about release or how to care for the butterfly or moth. It is best to do some research before introducing this insect to your environment. Many are not indigenous to the area and may damage the local balance.

Discussion

1. Which stage did you find most interesting? Explain why.
2. What other things go through cycles?
3. Did you think your caterpillar ate a lot of food? Explain.
4. What would happen if the food source for the larva were destroyed (pesticides, construction, weather)?
5. In which stages could you see a hint of how the next stage would look? [The wings can be seen in the chrysalis.]
6. What were the similarities and differences in the life cycles of the butterfly and the moth?

Assessment

Have students make a "film strip" of the life cycles of the butterfly and moth and write a narrative to accompany it. This can be used to assess the students' understanding of the metamorphoses of moths and butterflies.

Extension

Students can study the life cycles of other living things such as a tadpoles, mealworms, or silkworms.

Curriculum Correlation

Literature, Non-Fiction:

French, Vivian. *Caterpillar, Catapillar.* Candlewick Press. Cambridge, MA. 1993.

Gibbons, Gail. *Monarch Butterfly.* Holiday House. New York. 1989.

Ryder, Joanne. *Where Butterflies Grow.* Lodestar Books, Dutton. New York. 1989.

Watts, Barrie. *Butterfly and Caterpillar.* Silver Burdett. Englewood Cliffs, New Jersey. 1985.

Whalley, Paul. *Butterfly and Moth: An Eyewitness Book.* Alfred A. Knopf. New York. 1988.

Literature, Fiction:

DeLuise, Dom. *Charlie the Caterpillar.* Simon & Schuster. New York. 1990.

Howe, James. *I Wish I Were a Butterfly.* Gulliver Books. New York. 1987.

Home Link

Have students take their film strips home to share with their parents. Because of high interest, it may be a good time to schedule a family science night so parents can closely observe the project.

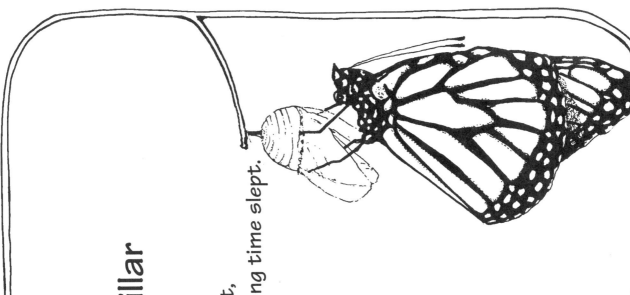

Roly Poly Caterpillar

By Barbara Ann Novelli

Roly poly caterpillar into a corner crept,

Made itself a sleeping bag and for a long time slept.

Resting, changing caterpillar

Woke up by and by,

Found itself with beautiful wings,

Turned into a butterfly!

Hand Motions

Line 1   Use fingers of one hand to crawl along other arm.

Lines 2 and 3   Close fist and circle other arm; stop circling and let fist rest on underside of arm.

Line 4   Begin to slowly move fingers in closed fist.

Lines 5 and 6   Lock thumbs and slowly open fingers to form a butterfly.

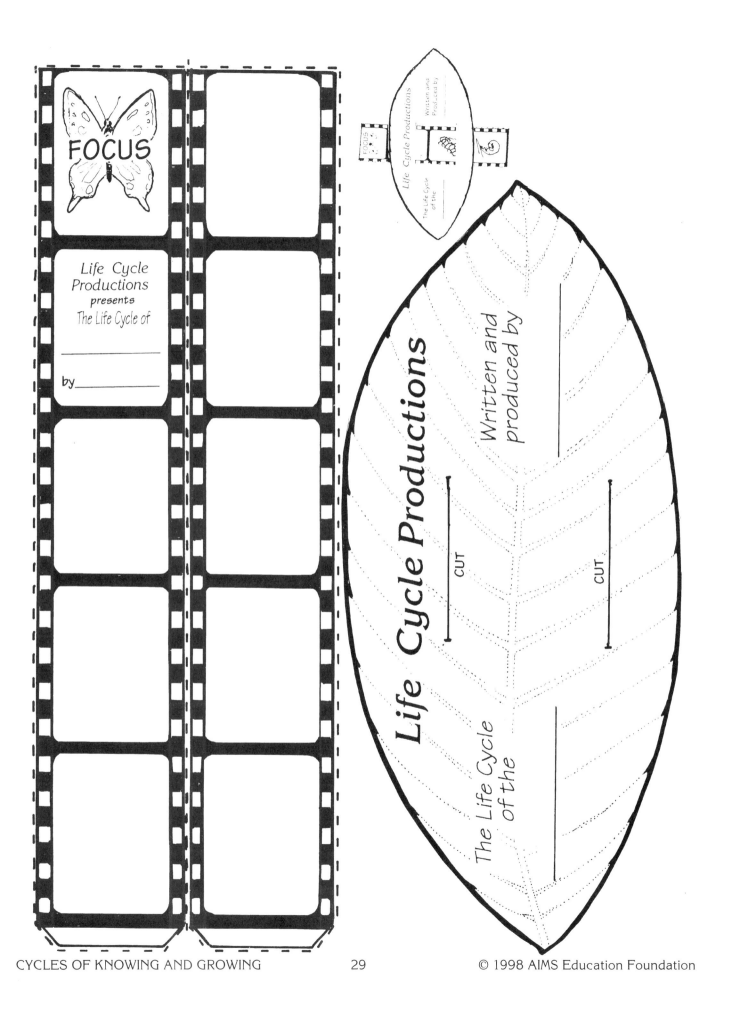

FOCUS

Life Cycle
Productions
presents
The Life Cycle of
_____

by_____

Life Cycle Productions

Written and
produced by

CUT

CUT

The Life Cycle
of the

Life Cycle Productions

The Life Cycle of the _____

Frame 1 _____

_____

_____

Frame 2 _____

_____

_____

Frame 3 _____

_____

_____

Frame 4 _____

_____

_____

Frame 5 _____

_____

Butterfly Cycle

Words by Suzy Gazlay   Tune: Row, Row, Row Your Boat

Hatch, hatch, lit-tle egg,
I'm so ver-y small.
Tee-ny ti-ny cat-er-pil-lar, you
can't see me at all.

Crawl, caterpillar, crawl,
Munching on a leaf.
Crawling, munching, crawling, munching,
Eat and eat and eat.

Form, form chrysalis
I'm a different shape;
Hanging by a silken thread
Until I can escape.

Rest, rest, chrysalis
While I change inside.
Now at last my time has come
To be a butterfly.

Stretch, stretch, pretty wings,
It's a special day.
Soon they will be strong enough
For me to fly away.

Fly, fly, butterfly,
Fly from flower to tree.
Find a place to lay my eggs
So they can grow like me.

This song is meant to be acted out as it is sung.
It can also be sung as a round.

Silkworms

Topic
Life cycle of silkworms

Key Question
How does a silkworm change over time?

Focus
Growth in the larval stage of an insect's life cycle

Guiding Documents
Project 2061 Benchmarks
- *A lot can be learned about plants and animals by observing them closely, but care must be taken to know the needs of living things and how to provide for them in the classroom.*
- *Animals eat plants or other animals for food and may also use plants (or even other animals) for shelter and nesting.*

NRC Standards
- *Plants and animals have life cycles that include being born, developing into adults, reproducing, and eventually dying. The details of this life cycle are different for different organisms.*
- *Employ simple equipment and tools to gather data and extend the senses.*

NCTM Standards
- *Construct number meanings through real-world experiences and the use of physical materials*
- *Make and use measurements in problems and everyday situations*
- *Collect, organize, and describe data*
- *Construct, read, and interpret displays of data*

Math
Measurement
Graphing
Estimating

Science
Life science
 life cycles
  insects

Integrated Processes
Observing
Predicting
Collecting and recording data
Comparing and contrasting
Generalizing

Materials
For the class:
 live silkworms (see *Management*)
 supply of mulberry leaves
 piece of silk (example: scarf)
 hand lenses
 thin or medium yarn

For each student:
 small container (see *Management*)
 sponge piece, optional (see *Management*)

Background Information
The silkworm (scientific name *Bombyx mori*) is the larval stage of a fairly large white moth. Like other moths, the silkworm moth goes through a *complete metamorphosis*, a process of changing into four very different stages: egg, larva, pupa, and adult moth.

Although many insects and spiders spin silk threads, the silk of the silkworm is one of the few that can be made into cloth economically. For this reason, silkworm moths are raised by people and are rarely found in the wild. Silkworms raised in silk factories lead a very protected life. The eggs are kept in cold storage until early spring. Then they are incubated for about 20 days until they hatch into a tiny (3 mm) 12-section, six-legged larva. The larvae are kept on clean trays and fed fresh mulberry leaves every two to three hours.

At first, the young silkworms eat almost continuously both night and day. During the larval stage, they will grow to nearly 70 times their original size, shedding their skins four times in the process. After the first molt, their appearance changes from black and somewhat hairy to greenish-white and smooth. Their appetite is voracious — a single silkworm can eat a large mulberry leaf, and the noise of an entire colony munching can be heard from several feet away. By the time a silkworm is ready to spin a cocoon, it will weigh more than 10,000 times as much as it did when it was first hatched.

When the silkworm is fully grown, it will stop eating and spin a cocoon. First it spins a web-like kind of net to attach itself to a twig or the side of the container. Then it swings its head side-to-side in a figure eight motion while two glands near the lower jaw give off a fluid which hardens into silk thread. The silkworm also produces a different gummy fluid which sticks the two strands of silk together. After as many as three days of spinning the silk around and around its body, the fluids are used up and the cocoon is complete.

Inside the cocoon, the larva changes into the third part of the life cycle, the pupa. It takes about three weeks for the pupa to turn into a moth. When the adult moth breaks out of the cocoon, it spits out a special liquid that dissolves the silk, making a large hole and breaking the long silk thread that formed the cocoon into many short ones. Because of this, most commercially-raised silkworms are killed during the pupa stage so the silk won't be ruined. Only a few moths are allowed to emerge, mate, and lay eggs to begin the life cycle again.

Management

1. These activities should be done in the spring or early summer when mulberry leaves are available. You will need a source of mulberry leaves to supply the silkworms with fresh food daily.

2. Each student will need a small box or other container with sides 7 – 0 cm (3 – 4 inches) high or more for their silkworm home. A copy paper box lid works well for housing a large number of silkworms. Eggs can be kept in a box or jar until they hatch.

3. Each silkworm home will need a fresh leaf each day (more when the silkworms are larger). Leaves in the individual homes will stay fresh longer if you keep them in an inch-square piece of sponge with a slit from the middle to one edge. Each day saturate the sponge with water and put the freshly cut stem of a mulberry leaf in the slit. Mulberry leaves will keep in a plastic bag in the refrigerator for several days.

4. The silkworms like branches or some other place to attach when they are ready to spin. If these are not provided, they may crawl out of the box looking for a more suitable place.

5. This activity may be done beginning with either eggs or larvae. If you begin with eggs, remember that they need three to four weeks to hatch from the time they are taken out of the refrigerator. If you are beginning with larvae, skip *Procedure 3* of *Part 1*.

6. When the silk moths emerge, put accordion-pleated construction paper in the habitat. The moths will lay their eggs in the pleats. Put the paper with eggs in a tightly sealed container.  Next spring, as soon as the mulberry trees are ready to sprout leaves, put the paper with eggs out in the silkworm homes at room temperature. In a few weeks you will have very small, very hungry silkworms ready to begin their life cycle again!

7. Most likely some silkworms will not survive. Plan for enough (in either individual or group habitats) to assure that each student will have several to work with.

8. Although the students should observe the silkworms on a daily basis, the measuring process is more effective if it is done only once or twice a week. Rate of growth depends on such things as amount of fresh food available and room temperature. You will need to take this into consideration, and adjust your graph accordingly.

9. Duplicate calendar pages for each month of observation. From egg hatching to egg laying usually takes about six to eight weeks.

10. Sources for silkworm eggs include:
    Insect Lore, P.O. Box 1535, Shafter, CA 93263 (1-800-LIVE BUG)
    Carolina Biological Supply Company, 2700 York Road, Burlington, NC 27215 (1-800-334-5551)

Procedure

Part 1: Introduction to Silkworms

1. Bring a piece of silk to class. Ast students where they think the silk came from. (If available read pages 2-9 of *Agatha's Featherbed* by Carmen Agra Deedy. Peachtree Publishers. Atlanta, GA. 1991.) Emphasize that the fibers in this cloth were made by an insect called a silkworm. Build upon prior knowledge about caterpillars and butterflies and their life cycle to help them make a connection between silkworms and silk moths.

2. Describe how silkworms are raised in factories. A book such as Sylvia Johnson's *Silkworms* or pictures from an encyclopedia will help. Explain that they are going to raise some silkworms in the classroom.

3. Show the students the silkworm eggs. Provide time for the students to examine the eggs using a hand lens. Place the eggs in a box in a central part of the room. Over the next few weeks, until the eggs hatch, encourage the students to keep a close watch and take note of and discuss any changes.

4. When the silkworms hatch, have the students make a calendar for the month, recording the dates for the month. Have students glue the birthday marker in the appropriate place on the calendar. Students can use the *Waiting* sticker for the days of the month prior to the hatching day. (When the silkworms hatch, you may want to celebrate the birth of the silkworms with a party.)

Part 2: Measuring the Growth of Silkworms

1. Discuss what silkworms need in order to grow strong and be healthy. Lead a discussion about an appropriate habitat to keep them in the classroom. If necessary, suggest some kind of box, as well as something on which to spin their cocoon.

2. Have each student build a habitat, sharing with other class members how it will meet the needs of a silkworm.

3. Inform the students that the calendar will be the observation log to keep a record of the changes in appearance of their silkworms. Tell them that there are special markers to note some significant events in the silkworm's life cycle which can be cut and placed on the day when those things happen. If desired, students can include observations of the silkworm's eating habits and various other descriptions, along with larger-than-life illustrations, in a journal.

4. Once a week (on the same day each week), have students record the length of the silkworm on the growth chart by cutting a strip of yarn, laying it alongside a representative silkworm, marking the length of the silkworm, and gluing or taping the yarn to the chart. Direct them to record their observations below the graph on the corresponding date.

Part 3: Measuring How Much a Silkworm Eats
1. After the silkworm has grown to at least two centimeters, challenge the students to try to find out how much it eats each day. Discuss the strategies they suggest.

2. Have each student choose a mulberry leaf that will fit on the grid paper and trace around it. Have them copy or cut it out double so they have two paper leaves. Direct them to put the real leaf and one silkworm in a separate container.

3. Wait an entire day, then tell them to put the remains of the leaf on one of the paper leaves and trace what is left. Have them cut the paper leaf so that it looks like the eaten leaf and compare it to the tracing of the original leaf. Direct them to glue or tape the two leaves side by side.

4. Have students repeat this every week or every few days with a similar-sized leaf and compare the results. (If the silkworm is large and the leaf is small, they may have to measure how much is eaten in a period of several hours.)

5. Debrief the silkworm study by having students bring their calendars and graphs to sharing time and present some of their favorite observations and days in the life of their silkworm.

Discussion
Part 1
1. Where have you noticed silk before? How do you think it is made?
2. What other animals can you think of that also spin silk?
3. Think about the life cycle of a silkworm. How is it like the life cycle of other animals? How is it different?
4. Explain how you made your habitat. How and why did you decide to build it this way?
5. What do you think is the best thing about your habitat?

Part 2
1. Did all the eggs hatch at the same time or on the same day? How do you explain this?
2. How would you describe your silkworm? Does it look like everyone else's?
3. Compare the length of your silkworm to others. Are they the same? Why do you think some silkworms might grow faster or slower than others?
4. Are there any changes you might make in your silkworm habitat or in the way you are caring for your silkworm that might help it grow faster? Explain your ideas.
5. After watching your silkworm grow for several weeks, how can you predict how long it will be in a week? ... in two weeks?

Part 3
1. How much did you predict your silkworm might eat? Why did you think so?
2. Have you been surprised to see how much silkworms eat? Why do you think they need to eat so much?
3. Were there other silkworms in the class that ate a lot more or a lot less than yours? How can you explain this?
4. Would you say that it is true that a silkworm eats its own weight in food every day? How do you know?
5. What other animals can you think of that eat close to their own weight in food every day?

Extension
Use the silkworms to set up different controlled experiments. Possibilities include: Which does a silkworm prefer, a younger leaf or an older leaf? ... a wet or a dry leaf? Use cutouts of the leaves to make a representational graph depicting the results.

Curriculum Correlation
Social Studies
Silk cloth has been an important part of China's history for several thousand years. Various Chinese legends and folktales contain fascinating stories illustrating the value of silk in the Chinese culture. Today silkworms are raised there commercially.

Literature
Silkworms by Sylvia Johnson (Lerner Publications, Minneapolis. 1982.) is an excellent resource book with outstanding photographs.

Language Arts
Have the students write or dictate a story about their silkworm home and why they designed it the way they did.

Home Link
Ask the students to look for objects made of silk and get permission to bring them to school to share.

Leaf Graph

Name

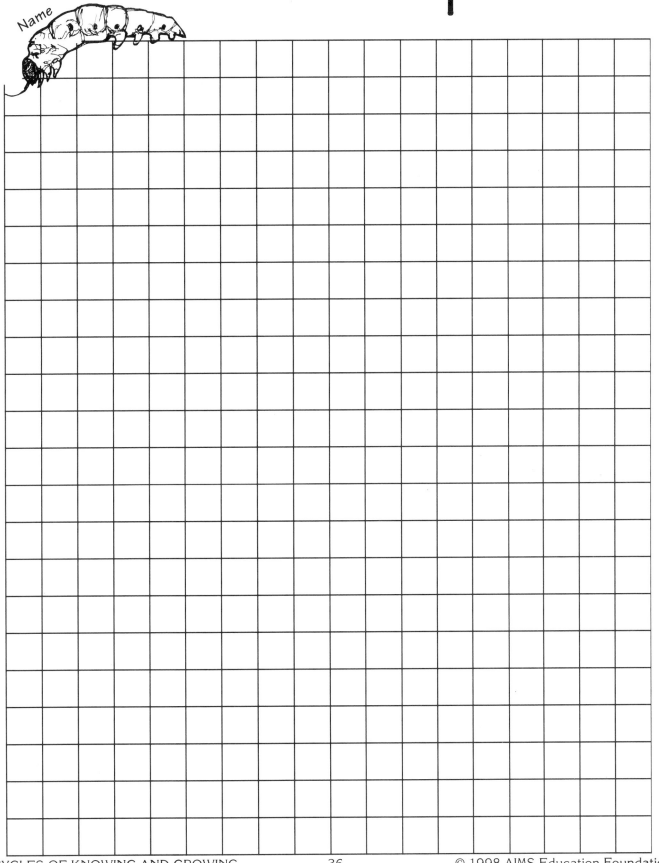

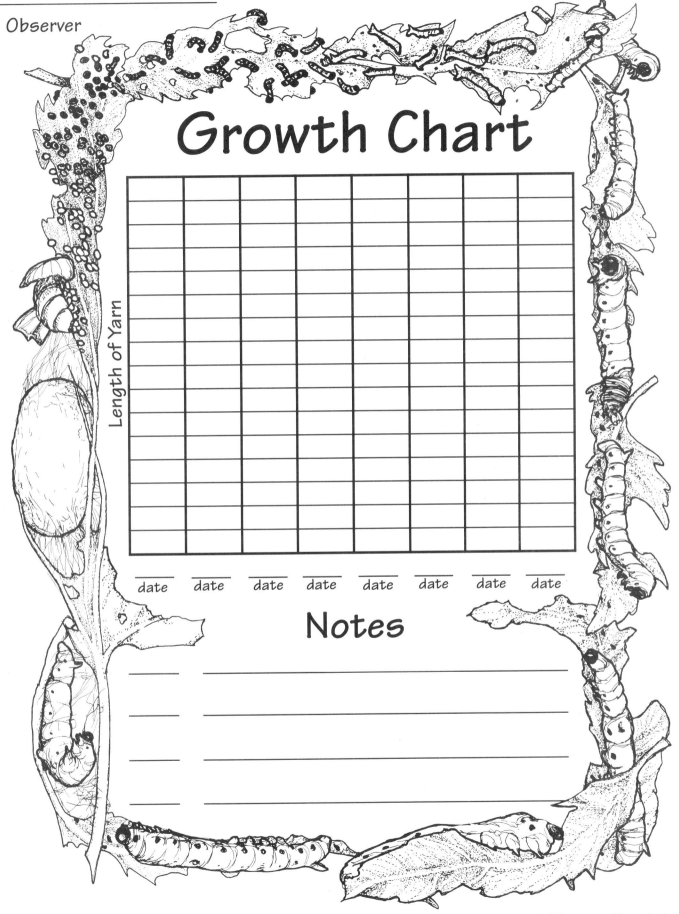

Observer _____

Growth Chart

Length of Yarn

date   date   date   date   date   date   date   date

Notes

_____
_____
_____
_____

My Silkworm Calendar

Month

Monday	Tuesday	Wednesday	Thursday	Friday

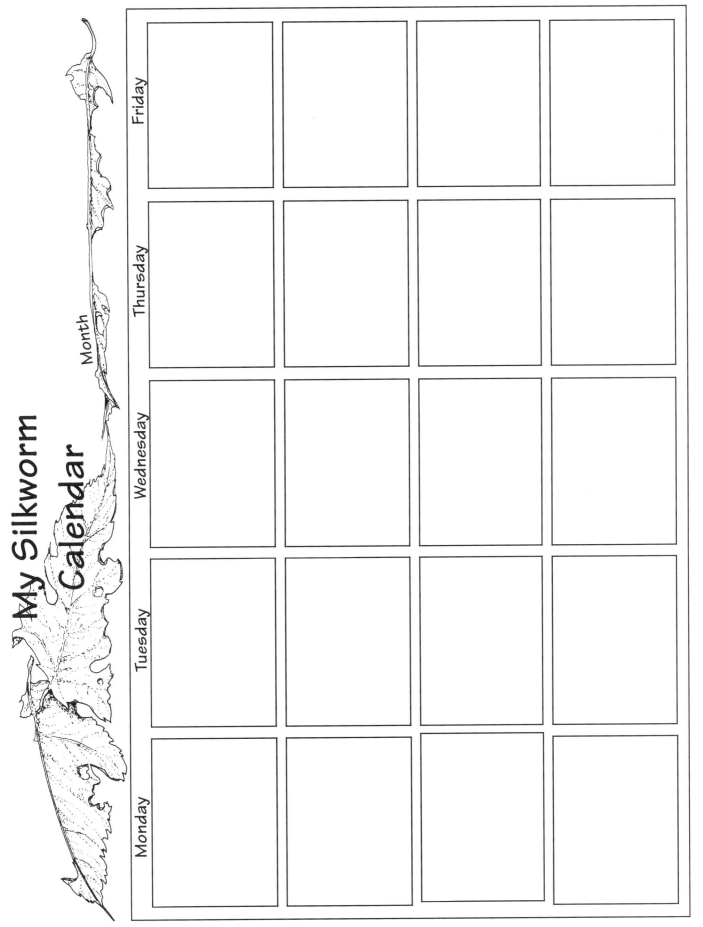

Calendar Cut-outs

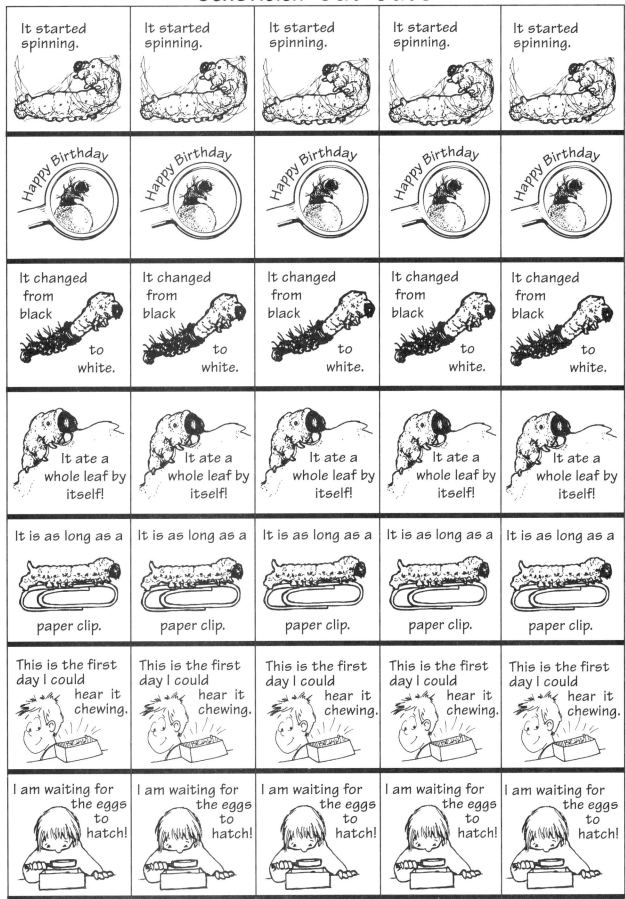

Just a Little Sprout

Topic
Plants: Life cycle of a pumpkin

Key Question
How does a pumpkin plant change as it goes through its life cycle?

Focus
Students will plant pumpkin seeds and observe the cycle of growth.

Guiding Documents
Project 2061 Benchmarks
- *A lot can be learned about plants and animals by observing them closely, but care must be taken to know the needs of living things and how to provide for them in the classroom.*
- *Change is something that happens to many things.*

NCR Standards
- *Simple instruments, such as magnifiers, thermometers, and rulers, provide more information than scientists obtain using only their senses.*
- *Plants and animals have life cycles that include being born, developing into adults, reproducing, and eventually dying. The details of this life cycle are different for different organisms.*

NCTM Standard
- *Make and use measurements in problem and everyday situations*

Math
Measuring
Ordering

Science
Life science
    life cycles
    change

Integrated Processes
Observing
Comparing and contrasting
Collecting and recording data
Communicating

Materials
For each student:
  3 pumpkin seeds (see *Management*)
  8-ounce transparent plastic cup
  potting soil to fill cup
  centimeter measurement strip (see *Management*)
  construction paper
  old newspaper
  bamboo skewer or twist tie, optional
  markers
  rubber band

For the class:
  extra seeds and cups
  permanent marker
  turkey baster

Background Information
In order to germinate, seeds must absorb water until they swell and burst their seed coat. Inside the seed is a tiny embryo, surrounded by stored food. The root is usually the first structure to emerge. It grows rapidly, absorbing water and minerals from the soil. Then the shoot begins to grow, pushing its way through the surface of the soil into sunlight. When the first leaves form, the plant begins to manufacture its own food.

When the small pumpkin plant in this activity receives what it needs, more leaves grow and vines spread out. Flowers then bloom on the vines and fruit begins to develop. This fruit, the pumpkin, matures. We can pick it off the vine, save the seeds, plant them, and continue the cycle.

Management
1. If you have previously carved a pumpkin and saved its seeds, these seeds can be used for this activity. However, it is suggested that you also purchase pumpkin seeds to plant because of the increased germination rate of the commercially produced seeds.
2. Cut a piece of construction paper slightly larger than the centimeter measurement strip. Mount the centimeter measurement strip onto the construction paper strip and label with each student's name. Beforehand or during the activity, tape each measurement strip vertically on the window or wall behind the surface (table or window sill) where the plantings will be kept. Space the strips so that a cup can be placed in front of each one. The bottom line of the strip should be approximately level with the top of the soil.
3. Prepare a planting station with cups, moistened soil, seeds, and a permanent marker to label the cups. Placing newspaper under the work area will help with the clean-up.
4. A turkey baster can help control the amount of water students use on their plants.

Procedure
1. Find out how much the students know by discussing the *Key Question*. After the discussion,

tell students they will be observing what changes occur after they plant the pumpkins seeds.

2. Demonstrate how to fill cups with the moistened soil and to plant seeds by placing one seed between the soil and the side of the cup, as illustrated. This will allow for observation of plant growth below the top of the soil. Show students how to poke the other seeds down into the soil. Place this cup under a growth strip labeled *Class Plant*.

3. Invite the students to work in pairs at the planting station. Encourage them to help each other as they plant their seeds in the cups. Direct the students to place their cups in front of the centimeter growth strips. Ask a few students to plant extras for the class or school garden.

4. Guide students each time they water the seeds. Explain that plants need enough water to grow, but that too much water is harmful. Show them how to use the turkey baster to water their seeds.

5. When the seeds begin to sprout, start measuring growth every day. Keep track on the centimeter growth strips by coloring in the bars to show how far the plant has grown since the last measurement; use a different color each time. As the pumpkin vines grow, facilitate measuring by gently lifting them or by staking them up with skewers.

6. As the plant grows, encourage students to report and compare their observations during a class meeting. Students can also record their observations in a journal.

7. Provide time for students to measure the plants' growth for about a week or until all cups have seedlings that can be transplanted. Wrap the growth strip around each cup and secure it with a rubber band. Read the transplanting instructions to the class. Send the plants and instructions home for transplanting. If there is a school garden, transplant the extra pumpkin plants in the garden.

8. Again, ask the students the *Key Question*. Allow time for a class discussion.

9. Have individual students make their predictions in *The Cycle of My Pumpkin Seed* cuff book. The book is made by cutting along the broken line, folding the cuff under, and stapling it at the ends. They then assemble the book so that the cuffs hold *Cycle Cards* inside.

10. After students have cut the *Cycle Cards* apart, direct them to place the cards in order in their cuff books. Allow them time to compare their order with their neighbor's and then as a class, discuss the life cycle of a pumpkin plant. Read one of the books listed in *Curriculum Correlation* to support this understanding.

11. Tell students you hope to see some of their mature pumpkins return to school next year.

Discussion
1. What happened to the seed? What does germinate mean?
2. Did all the seeds germinate? Why do you think they didn't all germinate?
3. Compare the rate of germination with your classmates.
4. What helped the seeds to grow?
5. If you could select anywhere to put your pumpkin seed, where would that be and why?
6. Describe in your own words the life cycle of a pumpkin.
7. Describe other living things that follow a similar cycle.

Extensions
1. Use Unifix cubes to measure the vine. Encourage students to find objects in the classroom equal in length to the vine that day.
2. Use different amounts of water on two different pumpkin plants and observe whether they develop differently.
3. Plan with the next year's teachers so they encourage students to bring the pumpkins they grew back to school to continue observing the cycle another year.
4. Suggest students take pictures of their pumpkin as it grows in their yard at home and bring them to school next year to share.

Curriculum Correlation
Literature

King, Elizabeth. *The Pumpkin Patch*. Dutton's Children's Book. New York. 1990.

Ray, Mary Lyn. *Pumpkins*. Harcourt Brace Jovanovich. San Diego. 1992.

Titherington, Jeanne. *Pumpkin, Pumpkin*. Scholastic, Inc. New York. 1986.

Home Link
1. After several verbal rehearsals with the cuff books, students may take them home and put them in order for their parents.
2. Transplant the seedlings at home.

Assessment
Have students write or dictate a narrative to accompany their cycle cuff book.

Name	Name	Name	Name
24	24	24	24
23	23	23	23
22	22	22	22
21	21	21	21
20	20	20	20
19	19	19	19
18	18	18	18
17	17	17	17
16	16	16	16
15	15	15	15
14	14	14	14
13	13	13	13
12	12	12	12
11	11	11	11
10	10	10	10
9	9	9	9
8	8	8	8
7	7	7	7
6	6	6	6
5	5	5	5
4	4	4	4
3	3	3	3
2	2	2	2
1	1	1	1

Put plants by a window. Tape strips beside the plants. Use a different color each day to record the growth of the plants.

CYCLES OF KNOWING AND GROWING

42

© 1998 AIMS Education Foundation

The Cycle of My Pumpkin

STAPLE

STAPLE

FOLD UNDER

STAPLE

- - - CUT - - -

STAPLE

FOLD UNDER

STAPLE

Date

Pumpkin Biologist

STAPLE

43

To make a pumpkin cycle book:
  1. Cut book and cycle cards on broken lines.
  2. Fold book cuffs towards the inside.
  3. Staple book and cuff ends.
  4. Place cycle cards in order.

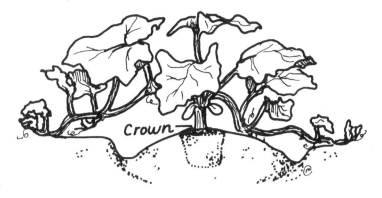

Crown

Dear Families,

Last fall when we used pumpkins in our classroom, we saved the seeds. This spring we planted our seeds, and since then we've been observing and recording the growth of our seedlings. I've encouraged the children to find a place to transplant their seedlings at home so that they too can become pumpkin farmers. Hopefully, the children will be able to return to school next year with pumpkins they started as seedlings in our class.

Here are the directions for transplanting:

1. Find a sunny spot which allows enough room for a vine to grow.
2. Remove the seedling from the cup, keeping as much soil around the roots as possible.
3. Plant the seedling into mounded soil so that the crown is even with the ground (see picture).
4. Leaving some soil around the crown of the plant, scoop out a ring of soil about one-half inch deep around the plant to form a basin. This will help keep water close to the plant's roots.

_____

Pumpkin Farmer (student)

_____

Teacher

Golden House

Topic
Decomposition: pumpkins

Key Question
How will a carved and uncarved pumpkin change over time?

Focus
Students will observe and keep a record of what happens to a pumpkin that has been carved.

Guiding Documents
Project 2061 Benchmarks
- *Change is something that happens to many things.*
- *Some changes are so slow or so fast they are hard to see.*
- *People can often learn about things around them by just observing those things carefully, but sometimes they can learn more by doing something to the things and noting what happens.*

NRC Standard
- *Plants and animals have life cycles that include being born, developing into adults, reproducing, and eventually dying. The details of the life cycle are different for different organisms.*

Science
Life science
  decompostition

Integrated Processes
Observing
Communicating
Collecting and recording data
Comparing and contrasting
Predicting

Materials
For the class:
  Mouskin's Golden House by Edna Miller
  2 pumpkins
  1 carving knife
  camera, optional

For each student:
  clipboard, optional (see *Management*)

Background
Decomposition is the breaking down or decaying of organic material. It is accomplished by organisms of decay such as bacteria and fungi. Carving the pumpkin, thereby exposing its insides to the agents of decay, will expedite the process.

Management
1. A wooded, or natural area, near school will provide an optimal environment for this activity.
2. If keeping the pumpkins outside is not possible, they can be kept on a window ledge inside the classroom.
3. This activity can be done without any association to Halloween. To do so, have the students cut open one pumpkin, remove the seeds, and the pulp. The pulp can then be cooked and used in pumpkin bread or other recipes. Using activities such as *A Pumpkin With Class* (*AIMS Newsletter*, Volume VI, Number 3) will result in a cut up pumpkin, and an experience in place value and seeds.
4. If clipboards are not available, students can use a book as a hard writing surface when doing the field observations. Clothespins or rubberbands can be used to hold the paper onto the book.

Procedure
Part 1: Literature
1. Read Edna Miller's *Mouskin's Golden House* to students, drawing special attention to the illustrations of the jack-o'-lantern as it decomposes. After discussing the story, ask the students what they think will happen to the class's carved pumpkin as it sits outside or on the window ledge. Make a list of their predictions.

Part 2: Activity
1. As a class, take the carved pumpkin and the whole pumpkin to the selected spot. After both pumpkins have been positioned side by side, take time to share as many observations as possible. A photograph might be taken at this time. Using the observation sheet, have the students sketch both pumpkins. When the students return to class they can color their sketches and write a sentence about each.

2. Return to the pumpkin site several times. During each visit, make as many observations as possible and record the changes on new copies of the observation sheet. If appropriate, continue to use photographs as a means to record the decomposition process. Ask the students to think of three words that describe the whole pumpkin and three words that describe the carved pumpkin. When they return to the room, invite the class to share the describing words and record these words on the board. Urge students to use these words in their description of the pumpkins.

3. Continue to observe the changes and record as frequently as you wish.

4. When bringing the activity to a close, have the students go back and read their observations and look at their sketches. Tell them to make a summary statement of the changes (or lack of changes) in both pumpkins.

5. Give each student a chance to read their summary statement to the class and then discuss how their statements were alike and different.

Discussion

Part 1: Literature

1. Why did the mouse choose the jack-o'-lantern for a house?
2. What is happening to the jack-o'-lantern?
3. What do you think will happen to the jack-o'-lantern after the end of the story?
4. Would the same changes take place in an uncarved pumpkin? How would changes be the same? ... different?

Part 2: Activity

1. What kinds of changes do you notice during the first visit? ... second visit? ... third visit?
2. Which part of the pumpkin changed first? Why?
3. What is causing these changes?
4. How long do you think it will take for the carved pumpkin to decompose completely? ... the whole pumpkin?

5. What happens to the parts of the decomposed pumpkin?
6. What do you think sped up the decomposition of the pumpkin?
7. Describe other things that you have seen change like the carved pumpkin.

Extensions

1. Bring several apples to school. Cut one into sections and leave the other intact. Observe the changes.
2. Leave an intact pumpkin in the classroom. Observe changes.
3. If photographs were taken, pin them up on a bulletin board. Invite students to sequence them through the decomposition process. Have them write captions for the photographs.

Literature

King Elizabeth. *The Pumpkin Patch.* Dutton's Children's Books. New York. 1990.

Miller, Edna. *Mouskin's Golden House.* Simon and Schuster. New York. 1964.

Ring, Elizabeth. *What Rot! Nature's Mighty Recycler.* The Millbrook Press. Brookfield, CT. 1996.

Rockwell, Anne. *Apples and Pumpkins.* Macmillan Publishing Co. New York. 1989.

Titherington, Jeanne. *Pumpkin, Pumpkin.* Scholastic, Inc. New York. 1986.

Home Link

Suggest to students that they find a place in their yard for their own carved pumpkin and observe changes.

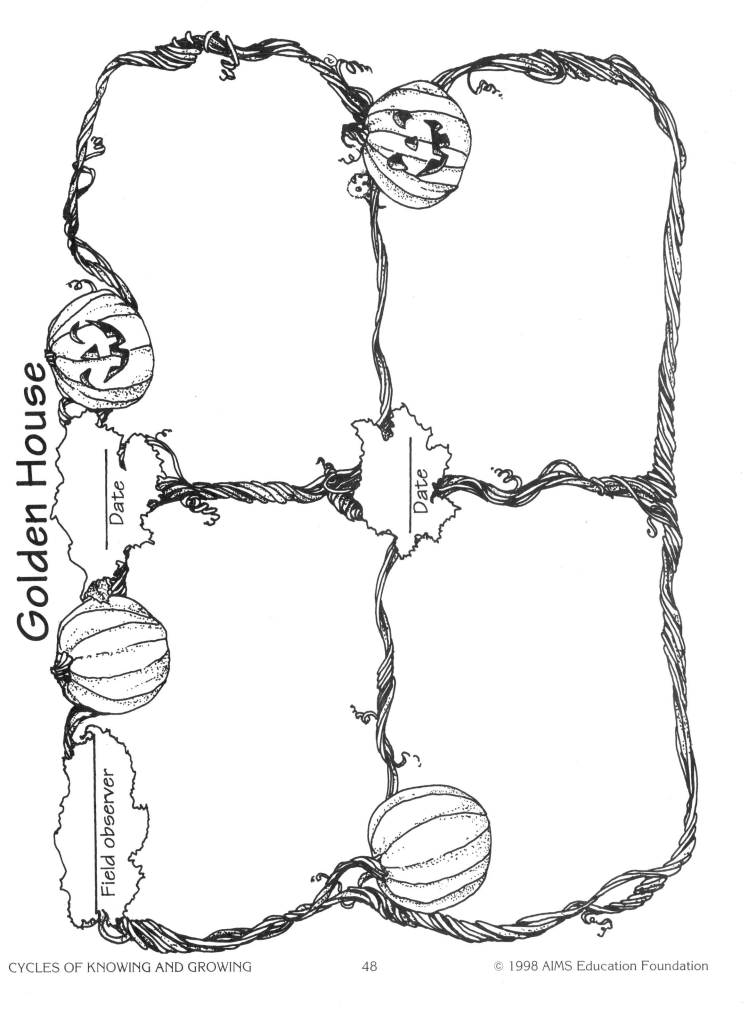

Golden House

Date _____

Date _____

Field observer

48

Pumpkin Song

Words by Suzy Gazlay

Tune: Did You Ever See A Lassie?

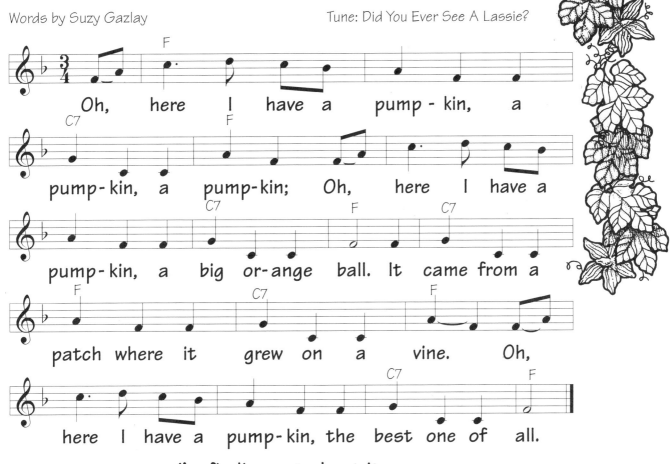

Oh, here I have a pump-kin, a pump-kin, a pump-kin; Oh, here I have a pump-kin, a big or-ange ball. It came from a patch where it grew on a vine. Oh, here I have a pump-kin, the best one of all.

I'm finding out about it,
　　　this pumpkin, my pumpkin.
I'm finding out about it, so I'll know it well.
I'm massing and measuring,
I'm counting its seeds,
I'm learning all about it;
　　　there's so much to tell.

Then maybe I will cook it,
　　　I'll cook it and eat it,
I could make it into cookies
　　　or a big pumpkin pie,
Or paint it, or carve it,
　　　A big Jack O'Lantern;
There's lots to do with
　　　pumpkins,
I think I will try.

Observing Bulbs

Topic
Plants: bulbs

Key Question
What can we learn about a bulb by carefully observing it?

Focus
Children will observe and describe the physical characteristics of a bulb.

Guiding Documents
Project 2061 Benchmark
- *Describing things as accurately as possible is important in science because it enables people to compare their observations with those of others.*

NCR Standard
- *Objects have many observable properties, including size, weight, shape, color, temperature, and the ability to react with other substances. Those properties can be measured using tools such as rulers, balances, and thermometers.*

Science
Life science
  physical characteristics of a bulb

Integrated Processes
Observing
Communicating
Comparing and contrasting
Collecting and recording data

Materials
For each child:
  daffodil bulb
  12" x 18" piece of yellow construction paper for making *My Bulb Observations* folder

For the class:
  large sheet of paper
  hand lenses
  daffodil bulb, cut in half

Background Information
During the growing season, the bulb's central bud section sends up a shoot which produces stem, leaves, and flowers above the ground. Roots grow downward from the solid basal plate of the bulb.

After flowering, food for the next season is manufactured in the foliage and stored in the fleshy, underground leaves. Parts of the plant above ground die. The outer scales form a dry and papery covering. At the beginning of the next growing season, the bulb sprouts and flowers.

CAUTION: Daffodil bulbs are poisonous if eaten. The Poison Control Center reports that an active ingredient is concentrated in the bulbs that when ingested can cause vomiting. In larger amounts, paralysis may occur.

Management
1. Beforehand, if possible, visit a nursery with your class. Make arrangements for daffodil bulbs to be set aside for students to choose and purchase. If this is not possible, buy bulbs and allow children to select from this collection. If appropriate, ask for a donation from parents to defray the cost of bulbs. Sometimes local nurseries will donate the bulbs.
2. Fold the yellow construction paper in half to make a folder. Glue a *My Bulb Observations* sheet to the front of each folder. This folder will be used to save all work connected with the activities *Observing Bulbs* and *Growing Bulbs*. Poetry will be copied onto the cover during the *Growing Bulbs* activity.

Procedure
1. As students examine their bulbs, brainstorm about specific attributes of the bulbs such as color, shape, texture, smell, etc. They should be told **never** to taste daffodil bulbs because they are poisonous.
2. Cut a bulb in half lengthwise to show the inside of a bulb. Point out the fleshy leaves, flower bud, and stem. Encourage students to touch and smell the inside of the bulb, but **never** to taste.
3. Model how to complete the *All About Bulbs* sheet. (The options for "Which way up?" are found on the *My Bulb* sheet. Have students cut apart the four options and glue their answer in the space

indicated on the *All About Bulbs* sheet.) Working together as a class, have students complete the activity sheet. If appropriate, have a brief discussion of plant needs before students complete the last section.

4. Place these papers in *My Bulb Observation* folders.

Discussion
1. What color are the bulbs?
2. Describe the texture of the bulbs.
3. Describe the smell of the bulbs.
4. What is the purpose of the thick, fleshy leaves of the bulb?
5. Where do the roots of the bulb grow?
6. How are bulbs like seeds? How are they different?

Extensions
1. Compare the daffodil bulb with other bulbs: edible (onions, garlic) and non-edible (tulip, hyacinth, crocus).
2. By what other attributes can our class set of bulbs be sorted?
3. Order bulbs by size.

51

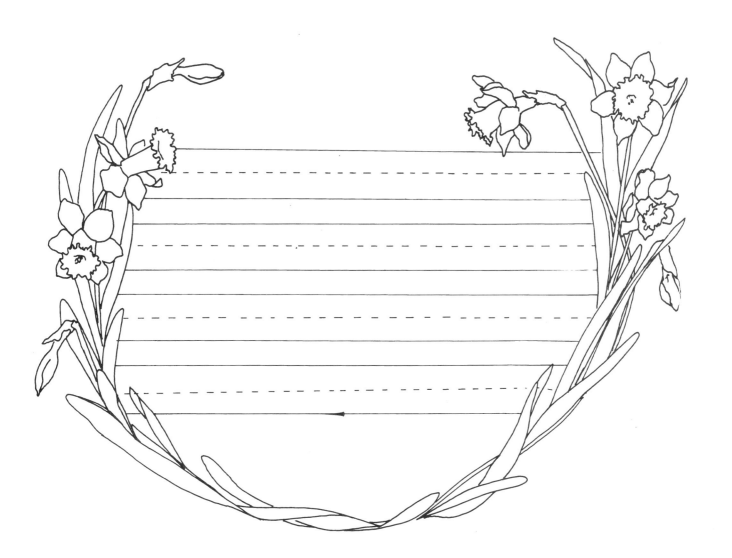

My Bulb Observations

_____

Observer

All About Bulbs

This is a picture of the outside of a bulb.

This is a picture of the inside of a bulb.

Which way up?

Glue picture showing the correct way to plant bulb.

What my bulb needs to grow...

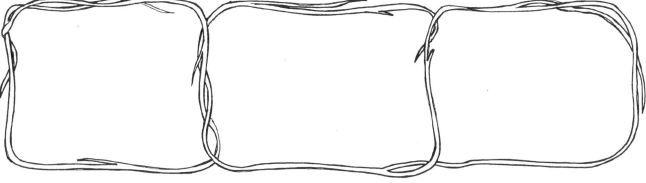

My Bulb

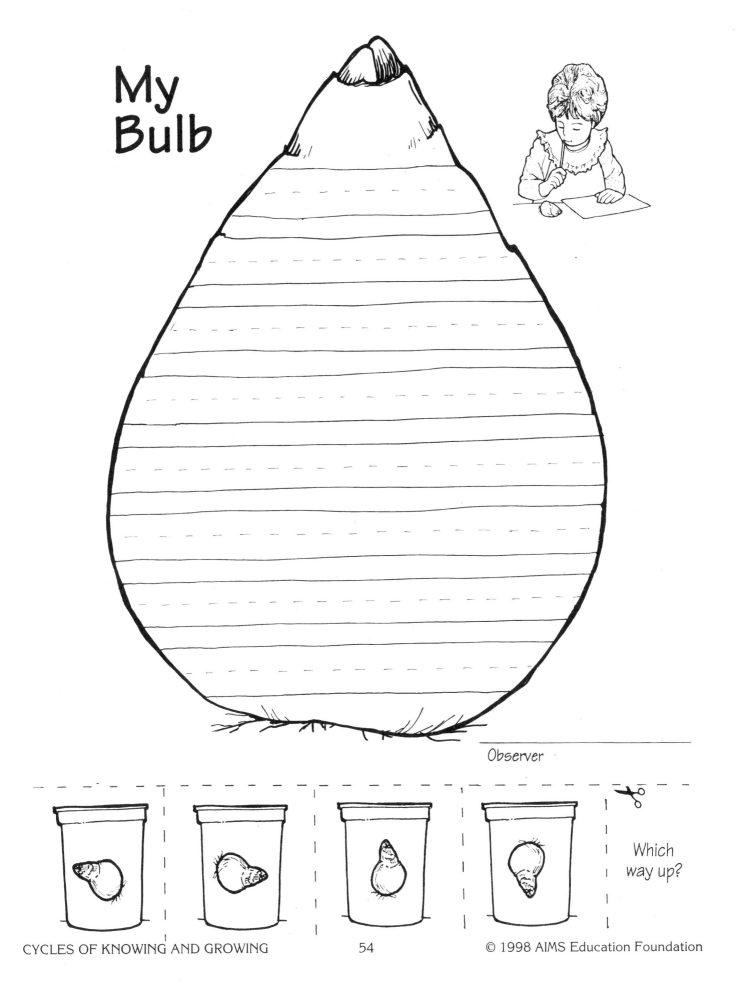

Observer

Which way up?

Growing Bulbs

Topic
Plants: bulb growth

Key Questions
What will happen to this bulb when we plant it in soil?
What will the bulb need to make it grow?

Focus
Children will observe the life cycle of a bulb.

Guiding Documents
Project 2061 Benchmark
* *Most living things need water, food, and air.*

NCR Standard
* *Plants and animals have life cycles that include being born, developing into adults, reproducing and eventually dying. The details of this life cycle are different for different organisms.*

NCTM Standards
* *Make and use measurements in problems and everyday situations*
* *Construct, read and interpret displays of data*

Math
Measuring
Graphing

Science
Life science
   plant growth

Integrated Processes
Observing
Recording
Comparing and contrasting

Materials
For each child:
   daffodil bulb (from *Observing Bulbs* activity)
   pot (at least 6 1/2" in diameter and 6-7" in height)
   My Daffodil Observations folder (from *Observing Bulbs* activity)

For the class:
   potting soil, approximately 2 cubic feet
   newspaper
   watering can
   poster board or transparency for making class graph

Background Information
See *Observing Bulbs.*

Management
1. Use bulbs either purchased or donated.
2. Select a time (usually between September and early November) for planting outside. Check with a nursery for the most appropriate time and planting conditions in your region. In colder climates, it is advisable to sink pots in the ground, whereas in warmer areas you may prefer to set the pots on a porch or patio. Check with a local nursery to determine in what type of conditions bulbs need to be stored.
3. Beforehand, prepare the class bulb graph on poster board or a transparency. The graph can be sketched or made into a transparency and enlarged using the overhead projector before tracing it. The graph should be approximately 12 by 18 inches.
4. When *Observing Bulbs* and *Growing Bulbs* are completed, the *My Bulb Observation* folders should contain three copies of the *My Observations* sheet:
   * first copy — done at school the day after planting
   * second copy — done at home about two months after planting
   * third copy — done when bulb is in full bloom.

Procedure
1. Lead the class in a discussion of the *Key Questions.* Discuss how these needs will be important considerations when both planting the bulbs and taking them home to watch them grow.
2. Have students in small groups at the planting center:
   * write their names on their pots
   * put several inches of soil in their pots
   * position bulbs, roots down, points up
   * cover the bulbs with soil
   * water the soil with a watering can.
3. After planting bulbs, have children write their names on the bulb graph in the first column to indicate that each has planted a bulb.
4. Discuss the best growing conditions for the bulb.
5. Send home bulb pots with first letter to parents.
6. The following day, using the first *My Observations* sheet, have children draw a picture of their pots and where they have placed them at home. Using frame sentences or "best-guess spelling,"

have students write a sentence or two about their bulbs — where they got them, what the bulbs need in order to grow, and where they put their pots at home.

7. File these observations in the *My Bulb Observations* folder.

8. Approximately two months into the growth cycle, send home the second copy of the *My Observations* sheet and the second letter of explanation to parents. Ask students to record their observations and return the activity sheet to school.

9. In class, discuss what they observed about their plants. File the *My Observations* sheets in the *My Bulb Observations* folders.

10. As students observe the bulbs sending up shoots of green, have them record their names in the second column on the class graph. This will indicate they have observed a shoot of green.

11. When their bulbs bloom, have them record their names on the class graph in the third column. Encourage them to bring the blooming plants back to school for a visit and to share information about their daffodils.

12. Have students take the plant home with the third *My Observations* sheet and also with the third letter to parents. Tell the students to complete the sheet and bring it back to school.

13. When the sheet comes back to school, place it in the *My Bulb Observations* folder. Those students whose bulbs did not bloom should also write a final observation.

14. Teach the following poem and have students copy it on the cover of their *My Bulb Observations* folders:

> *A little yellow cup,*
> *A little yellow frill,*
> *A little yellow star,*
> *And that's a daffodil!*
> *(Author unknown)*

15. Once all the observations have been made, send the folders home.

Discussion

1. Describe what happened to your bulb.
2. What helped your bulb grow? Why do you think some did not grow?
3. What is the most important thing you learned when growing your bulb?
4. How can you use this information?

Extensions

1. Keep a daffodil in the classroom to observe what happens after it blooms. When leaves have yellowed, dig it up to observe. Does it look different from before planting?
2. After the bulbs have been removed from the soil, place them in **dated** paper bags, and send them home. If they are hung in a garage or other dry place, they will be ready for replanting next year.

Home Link

Encourage parents to participate in this activity by helping students both grow and observe the bulb as well as write about their observations.

My Observations

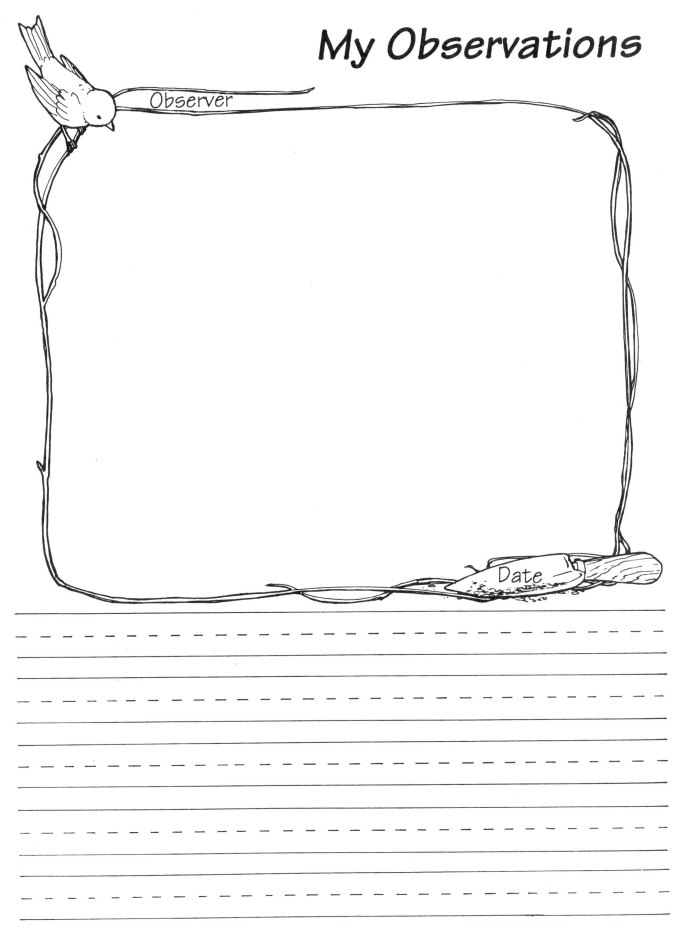

Observer

Date

Dear Families,
Your child planted a wonderful daffodil bulb today. We've talked about what our bulbs need to grow so that they will bloom in the spring. Will you please help find a spot in your yard or porch for the pot where the sun and rain will find it? We will be charting the growth of the plant by writing our observations throughout the cycle, so please encourage your child to care for the plant and to watch for any changes.

Thank you for your support of this project.

_____
Teacher

Bulbs are buried deep, deep, deep.
In the soil they sleep, sleep, sleep.
Yellow sunbeams bright, bright, bright.
Raindrops falling light, light, light.
Gentle breezes blow, blow, blow.
Little bulbs begin to grow, grow, grow.

(first letter)

Dear Families,

I've asked the children to keep track of the daffodil bulbs that they planted in the fall. They have written a "scientific" report once on what they have noticed, and I'm asking them to write another report based on their observations of the bulb growth. This time I am asking students to do their reports at home. Will you please encourage your child to use the special observation sheet to draw a picture of the plant as it looks now and then write at least two sentences about what has been observed? Students may use best-guess spelling and/or get help from you. Here are some ideas the children might find useful in deciding what to report:

- Does the bulb have "shoots of green"?
- How many shoots does it have?
- How tall is the biggest shoot?
- Does the plant have any buds or flowers?
- What helped your plant grow?

If your child's bulb has not sprouted, encourage him/her to record this, too. I've told the children that when their daffodil blooms, they may bring it to school for a visit. Thanks for your help.

_____
Teacher

(second letter)

Dear _____

Now that your daffodil has bloomed, please draw a picture of what it looks like again. Then write at least two sentences about what you observed. This time think about these questions.:

– When did you notice that your daffodil had bloomed?

– How many flowers does your plant have?

– How tall is your plant?

– What color are the flowers?

– What do you think will happen next?

When you return this observation to school, we will add it to your "My Bulb Observations" folder.

_____
Teacher

(third letter)

What a Corny Life

Topic
Life cycle of corn

Key Questions
Part 1: How would you describe your ear of Indian corn?
Part 2: How does your ear of Indian corn change over time?

Focus
Students will observe and compare the visual attributes of Indian corn and then place a cob in water and observe how it changes over several weeks.

Guiding Documents
Project 2061 Benchmarks
- *Change is something that happens to many things.*
- *People can keep track of some things, seeing where they come from and where they go.*

NRC Standard
- *Plants and animals have life cycles that include being born, developing into adults, reproducing, and eventually dying. The details of this life cycle are different for different organisms.*

NCTM Standards
- *Understand our numeration system by relating counting, grouping, and place-value concepts*
- *Collect, organize and describe data*
- *Make and use measurement in problem and everyday situations*

Math
Estimating
Measuring
Counting by tens

Science
Life science
    plants
        life cycle

Integrated Processes
Observing
Comparing and contrasting
Communicating
Predicting

Generalizing

Materials
For each pair of students:
    a dry ear of Indian corn (miniature or regular)
    clear plastic shoe box or similar container
    hand lenses
    balance
    non-customary units of mass: tiles, washers, marbles, Teddy Bear Counters
    dull dinner knife for removing kernels
    6 strips of green construction paper, 3 cm x 10 cm

For the class:
    3 ears of dry Indian corn
    chart paper
    3 one-liter bottles filled with water

Background Information
The many varieties of corn (or maize) can be grouped into seven major kinds: dent, flint, sweet, popcorn, waxy, and pod. These classifications are based chiefly on the characteristics of the kernels. What we call Indian corn is usually either flint or flour corn. Both types have hard, round kernels with smooth coats.

Flint corn is grown in Asia and Europe. as well as North, Central, and South America. In the U.S. it grows in the cooler climates in areas such as Wisconsin, Michigan, and New England. Since it has a short germination period, it can mature in the short growing season. Kernels range in color from white to deep red. Flint corn is used as food for people and livestock, as well as for decoration.

Flour corn, a very old variety, is grown in South Africa, as well as the Southwestern U.S. As the name implies, it has been used mainly for flour. Kernels have a wide range of colors, including dark blue.

A kernel of mature corn is a seed with three main parts:

seed coat: protects
endosperm: stores the starch and other food energy
embryo: develops into a new plant

When the corn is removed from the water and it lacks the nutrients it needs, growth will stop and decomposition will begin. Decomposition is the breaking down or decaying of organic matter. It is accomplished by organisms of decay, such as bacteria and fungi.

Management

1. This is a two part activity. In *Part 1* students observe and examine the dry corn and count the number of kernels in one ear. In *Part 2* of the activity, students will place a cob of Indian corn in water and observe and measure its growth while comparing it to a dry ear of corn and an ear of corn planted in soil and watered.

2. A dull dinner knife will help dislodge the kernels of Indian corn for counting sets of ten. If you wish to keep each set of ten separate, portion cups or plastic bags will help.

3. *Part 2* is best done in pairs.

4. Miniature Indian corn works well.

5. The corn takes 10-14 days to sprout in water. Drain and replace the water every two to three days. The corn will continue to grow in the water for three to four weeks after sprouting.

6. Prior to the activity, cut the 3 cm x 10 cm strips of construction paper for student books. Students should measure sprouts every three to five days. Have them measure only one of their sprouts. This will serve as reference for the growth of the other sprouts.

7. Throughout the activity, emphasize the three environments: whenever students check the growth of the corn in **water**, be sure they also check the corn in **soil** and **air**, even through the decomposition phase. Students should stop watering the cob in soil during the decomposition phase. The decomposition phase is powerful and should not be excluded.

8. The students can do the actual construction of the book while kernels are being removed in *Part 1*. To assemble the book, students need to first cut apart the pages along the broken line. They next need to cut out the peek hole slots along the broken lines. Have them then order the pages with the narrowest page on top and the widest page on the bottom. Staple along the left edge.

Procedure

Part 1

1. Encourage students to use hand lenses to observe the dry ear of corn.

2. Direct each student to remove one kernel of corn for closer observation.

3. Provide time for students to share their observations and as they are sharing, record their observations on the board.

4. After the sharing session, allow students adequate time to first glue their kernel on the cover of their book and then record their own observations about the cob of corn and kernel on page 1.

5. Tell them to look carefully at the colors and patterns of the Indian corn and color the picture to match their own cob of corn.

6. If a balance is available, encourage students to use it to obtain the mass of the dry cob of corn. This information can be added to page 1 of their book.

7. Hold up an ear of Indian corn and ask the class to make an estimate of how many kernels there are on the entire ear. Record all of the estimates.

8. Pass the corn around the room, giving each student a chance to remove ten kernels using the dull knife.

9. When each student has removed ten kernels, hold up the ear to show how many kernels remain on the cob. Count by tens (each student has ten kernels) until the class has determined how many kernels have been removed. Allow students to revise their estimates and then continue having each child remove a set of ten.

10. When all kernels have been removed, count by tens again starting with the previous total. Discuss the total number of kernels, including the number of tens and ones. For example, 42 tens and 7 single kernels would total 427.

Part 2

1. Once the students have completed their observations on the first page of the book, give each pair of students a plastic container in which to place their cob of corn. Help them fill the plastic tray with water until half of the corn is covered.

2. Bring students to a group-gathering place after each group has set up their cob of corn in a water environment. With the students watching, bury another ear of corn in soil and water it. Place the remaining cob in an empty container.

3. Ask the students the *Key Question* and record their ideas on chart paper. Ask students to think about the different containers and discuss what results they expect in each container. Tell them that they will continue to compare their cob in water with the cobs in soil and air.

4. When the first sprouts are visible, have students measure them with the construction paper strip by placing the piece of paper beside the sprout and cutting it the same height as the first sprout. They should glue this above the kernel on page 2 of their book. Direct students to also observe the cobs in soil and air only. They should also record the date as well as observations on page 2.

5. Repeat the observing, measuring, and comparing procedures several more times over the course of the three weeks.
6. Continue to change and add water until the sprouts begin to fall over. At this time remove the water from the containers, so the corn is no longer receiving any water at all. Direct students to continue to watch as the sprouts die and the ears begin to decompose.
7. Students should use the last page of the book to record three statements about the decomposing sprouts and corn.

Discussion
Part 1
1. How do the kernels differ from each other? How are they alike?
2. What strategies did you use when estimating the number of kernels of corn? Did you need to change your estimate once we started counting the kernels? Explain.
3. What are some ways we use corn?
4. How do you like to eat corn?

Part 2
1. What part of the corn grew?
2. How did the rest of the cob change?
3. How did the growth of corn in water compare with the one in air? … soil?
4. Compare the growth in each part of the corn. Which part of the corn changed first? … the most?
5. Did your corn grow at different rates during the three weeks?
6. How does your corn's growth compare with other corn in the class?
7. What did you learn when you were growing Indian corn?
8. What did you like best about this experience?

Extensions
1. As a class, plant an ear of sprouting Indian corn in soil and watch to see if it will continue to grow.
2. Lay a kernel of Indian corn on a moist paper towel, and place a second piece of moist towel over it. Daily remove the top towel and observe changes. Have students sketch the kernel every few days. The towels should be moist but not soggy.
3. Provide the balance and compare the mass of the wet and dry corn.
4. Try growing other types of corn.
5. Grind some loose kernels in a food grinder and compare the meal with processed cornmeal.

Curriculum Correlation
1. Make corn bread, cornmeal pancakes, or tortillas.
2. Make a chart of corn uses.
3. In art have students make drawings of Indian corn by tracing around a cob of Indian corn. Give students several colors of tempera and allow them to dip their index fingers in various colors and print with their fingers to look like kernels on the cob. When the pictures are dry, staple torn strips of brown paper bag or real corn husks to the base of the printed corn cob.

Literature
Aliki. *Corn is Maize*. Harper Row. New York. 1976.
Arnosky, Jim. *Raccoons and Ripe Corn*. Mulberry Books. New York. 1992.
de Paola, Tomie. *The Popcorn Book*. Scholastic, Inc. New York. 1978.
Hamilton, Virginia. *Drylongso*. Harcourt Brace Jovanovich. New York. 1992.

This is how my corn looks now.

I'll tell you about my corn....

This is how my corn looked after its sprouted.

Growing Indian Corn

by _____
date

I'll tell you about my corn....

cut out

cut out

I'll tell you about my corn...

cut out

This is how my
corn looks now.

cut out

This is how my corn looks now.

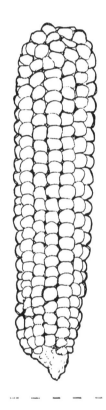

I'll tell you about my corn...

67

A Snap of Time

Topic
Seasonal changes in trees

Key Question
How does a tree change during the school year?

Focus
Students will adopt a tree for the school year and observe the changes in various aspects of the tree.

Guiding Documents
Project 2061 Benchmarks
- *Change is something that happens to many things.*
- *Some changes are so slow or so fast they are hard to see.*
- *People can keep track of some things, seeing where they come from and where they go.*

NRC Standard
- *Plants and animals have life cycles that include being born, developing into adults, reproducing and eventually dying. The details of this life cycle are different for different organisms.*

NCTM Standard
- *Collect, organize and describe data*

Math
Measurement

Science
Life science
    seasonal changes

Integrated Processes
Observing
Comparing and contrasting
Communicating
Collecting and recording data
Predicting
Generalizing

Materials
Clipboards or books and clothespins
Yarn
Hand lenses

Background Information
Watching a tree can give us a glimpse of seasonal changes. Most broadleaf trees lose their leaves in the fall when the amount of sunlight diminishes and the days become cooler. In contrast, conifers lose their needles only every three to four years. However, even with conifers, seasonal changes can be seen below the tree.

Trees produce seeds at certain times of the year. The seeds fall, absorb moisture, and finally some seeds germinate to produce new trees if conditions are right. In colder climates, the growth of a tree slows down during the fall and winter.

It is important for the observer to look for seasonal changes below and around the tree as well as looking at the changing tree. The soil and soil covering below the tree can change and therefore support us in noticing seasonal changes.

In the spring buds are visible on the tree and we begin to see new leaves. At that time, we will also most likely see new grass, small flowers, and the soil will feel warmer under the tree. While the tree remains green for most of the summer, the soil and plant life under it may start to dry. In fall and winter, leaves of a deciduous tree will change color and drop, covering the ground. In the winter the tree may be bare, and the grass and plant life below the tree may be dormant. Winter may bring frost or snow with the ground becoming cold and unpenetrable. Dead leaves may cover the ground. Because a tree can be a life support system for various animals, the animals associated with the tree may change as the seasons change.

Management
1. It will be very important that the adopted trees show seasonal changes during the school year. If a student is adopting a tree in his or her neighborhood, send a letter to parents encouraging them to help select a tree which will change during the seasons and be easily observable all year long. If the trees being adopted are on or near the school grounds, walk the area and select a spot that will optimally provide enough trees for each pair of students.
2. If this activity is done at school, it is best done in partners.
3. This activity will be most effective if it is started at the very first of the year so students will see the most change in their tree. At least once during each season, have the students do a formal observation.
4. Field recording can be difficult. The use of clipboards or books with clothespins used to keep the paper in place can make outdoor recording easier.

Procedure

1. Read *The Seasons of Arnold's Apple Tree* by Gail Gibbons. Tell the students they too are going to watch a tree for the school year. Ask them what they know about trees and how they change.

2. Take students on a walk to observe trees on the school grounds and the neighborhood. If possible include some information during your walk about trees that obviously change and those that do not. If they are going to adopt trees at school, have partners select their trees and sketch them. A strategy which will help them observe and sketch better is to look a little, sketch a little; look a little, sketch a little. When students are done, they should trade pictures with their partners and give each other suggestions about possible additions to their sketches.

3. Wait only a day or two and visit the trees again. This time make the close-ups sketches and data collection in relation to things they might see *on* or *under* the bark, *in* and *on* the branches and leaves, and *around* the roots and earth *below*. Have students touch the ground and discuss the warmth or coolness of the soil, as well as observe and make a record of the things growing or laying on the soil. They should look carefully at the bark around the base of the tree.

4. When students visit the tree the second time, have each partner select a branch and tie a piece of colorful yarn on a branch. Tell them they should look very carefully at the branch and its leaves each time they observe their tree. Encourage them to count the leaves, describe the color, smell the leaves and branches, and touch them.

5. While they are sketching, have the students also look for any living things that may be using the tree. It is important that a hand lens be used when looking at the tree bark, leaves, and critters. Have the students make a quick sketch of the critter.

6. Encourage a "silent observation" period while the students are visiting the tree. Direct students to sit near their trees and to remain quiet for a least one minute.

7. After the silent observation, allow time for students to share what they observed. Discuss the fact that looking is only one way to learn about their tree; listening, smelling, and touching also give us much information.

8. Each time the students visit their trees, continue to encourage them to sketch each part of the tree and its immediate environment as well as to make field notes of their observations. (Younger learners can dictate their observations as well as draw them.)

9. If appropriate, students can collect a fallen leaf or a twig to include in their album of their adopted tree.

10. To obtain a print of the leaf or bark, have the students do a rubbing or a printing. (See *Leaf Printing* in the AIMS publication *Budding Botanist*.)

Discussion

1. How has your tree changed?
2. Describe the changes in the branches of your tree over the adoption period. ... the ground. ... the bark. ... the inhabitants of your tree.
3. What kind of things lived in, on, and above the tree? Were any in all three places?
4. How do you feel about your tree now compared to when you first adopted it?
5. How did having a partner in this project help you learn about your tree?
6. What was your favorite time to observe your tree? What made it your favorite time?

Extensions

1. Invite an amateur photography group or the high school photography class to take pictures of the students and their trees several times during the year.
2. Invite a local forester or visit a local nursery to learn more about trees.
3. Write the National Arbor Day Foundation for information:

   > The National Arbor Day Foundation
   > 100 Arbor Avenue
   > Nebraska City, NE 68410

4. If your school has computers which are connected to some form of communication system such as Internet, write other schools and invite them to do this activity and share their observations so comparisons can be made.

Curriculum Correlation

Literature
   Gibbons, Gail. *The Seasons of Arnold's Apple Tree.* Harcourt Brace Jovanovich. New York. 1984.

Language Arts
   Have students write a frame poem about their tree. This is done by having the class generate all the words they can think of about the trees they are observing while the teacher records this word bank on the chalk-board. Direct the students to select from these words and to place them in the format shown below to write their poem.

My tree,

_____, _____

_____, _____

_____, _____

My tree!

Older students can be encouraged to use only adjectives in the blanks.

Physical Education
    Have students play Tree Tag. Direct the class to label or mark trees in some descriptive way. Then have someone (teacher or student) name or describe a tree and all students run to that tree. The person that is "it" tries to tag the runners. If he or she does, the tagged person becomes "it."

Assessment
    Demonstrate how to make the *Pyramid Diorama* and then give each student four copies of the page. Have them put the pages together as directed. In each of the segments, have students depict their tree during each season of the year. They can use construction paper and collage materials to create the seasonal changes above, in, on, and below the tree during the winter, summer, spring, and fall of the year. Students should then be interviewed to explain the changes in their tree. This interview can be video recorded or tape recorded. Students should be expected to include seasonal changes in relation to the tree and connect these changes to the changes in the weather.

Home Link
    This activity can be done at home.

CERTIFICATE OF ADOPTION

I hereby certify that this_____tree has been lovingly adopted by_____ on this ___day of _____in the year_____.

Signed,

_____
Teacher

_____
Adoptive parent

My tree in the
Winter

My tree

Close up of a branch

Close up of the bark

The ground under my tree

My tree in the Spring

Close up of a branch

Close up of the bark

My tree

The ground under my tree

My tree in the Summer

Close up of a branch

Close up of the bark

My tree

Lemonade 10¢

The ground under my tree

My tree in the Fall

Close up of the bark

Close up of a branch

My tree

The ground under my tree

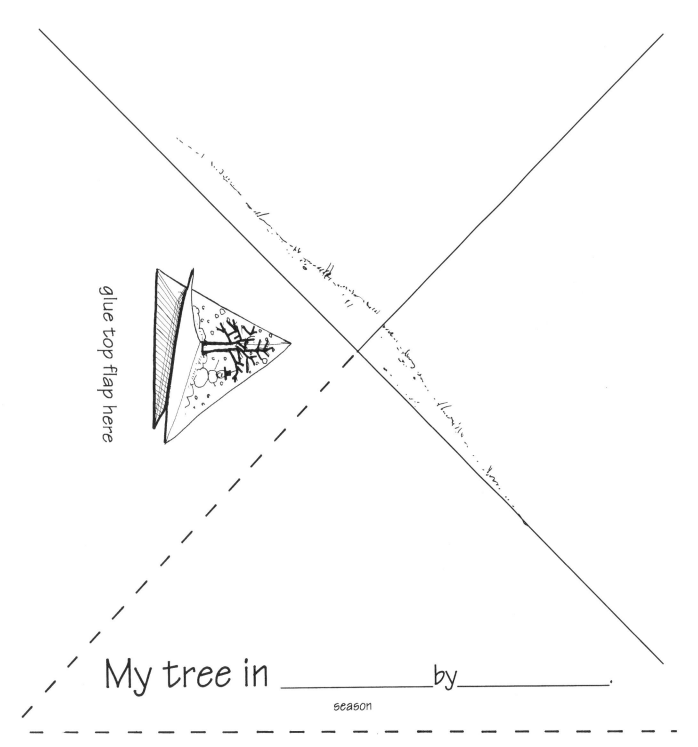

glue top flap here

My tree in _____ by _____.

season

Pyramid Diorama

Cut out along broken lines.
Fold along solid lines.
Draw a picture of your tree on the top triangles.
Fold flap over and glue.
Make one for each season.

Season-O

Topic
Seasonal changes above, on, and below the tree

Key Question
As the seasons change, what observations of the tree and its surroundings can you make?

Focus
Students will play a game which focuses on seasonal changes in relation to a tree.

Guiding Documents
Project 2061 Benchmarks
- *Change is something that happens to many things.*
- *Some changes are so slow or so fast they are hard to see.*
- *People can keep track of some things, seeing where they come from and where they go.*

NRC Standard
- *Scientists use different kinds of investigations depending on the questions they are trying to answer. Types of investigations include describing objects, events, and organisms; classifying them; and doing a fair test (experimenting).*

NCTM Standard
- *Collect, organize and describe data*

Math
Positional words

Science
Earth science
    seasons
Life science
    trees

Integrated Processes
Observing
Comparing and contrasting
Communicating

Materials
Game board and game pieces (see *Management*)

Background Information
    Seasonal changes in many areas are very dramatic but often are not carefully observed by the young learner. The activities, *Fallen Leaf* and *A Snap of Time*, have the students looking at the changes in an adopted tree over the school year and hopefully during the summer. In *Fallen Leaf* they look at one part of a tree, the leaf, and at the changes that occur after the leaf falls to the ground. In *A Snap of Time*, the students look at seasonal changes on and around a tree. In this activity they apply and extend their learning about seasonal changes by playing a game.

Management
1. It is important that the students have experienced the activity *A Snap of Time* before playing *Season-O* so they have some understandings about seasonal change.
2. *Season-O* is played much like the game Bingo in which the winner completely fills in a vertical, horizontal, or diagonal line. Copy the game pieces (seasonal markers) and game board (tree) on two different colors of paper so the win lines will be more evident.
3. Students can play this game in partners or groups of four. The teacher can also enlarge the game board and game pieces so the whole class can play (see *Procedure*). If you wish to play this as a whole class, the game pieces and game board need to be enlarged. The game board should then be placed on a bulletin board where the class can see it. Put a pin in the top center of each grid of the game board. Each team (half of the class) will need a different colored set of game pieces. These game pieces should have a hole punched in the top center of the piece so they can be placed easily over the pin on the game board. Each half of the class will take turns drawing a game piece and putting it on the game board as well as describing what season the game piece depicts and justifying their selection. The first team (half of the class) that gets their color pieces in a horizontal, vertical, or diagonal row wins.
4. Enlarge the book, *My Tree, My Tree, All Year Long*, to make a big book.

Procedure
1. Motivate the discussion of seasonal changes by reading *My Tree, My Tree, All Year Long*. After reading the book, ask students what changes they have observed in their tree over the year. Record their observations on chart paper or chalkboard which has been divided into four columns labeled *Winter, Summer, Spring*, and *Fall*.
2. Hold up the game board (or make a transparency and place it on the overhead projector) and ask

what the tree might look like in the winter. Discuss what the pictures might be above, on, and below the tree. Hold up (or place on the overhead) several game pieces and discuss where they would go on the tree. Encourage students to use descriptive language which helps them visualize the tree in the different seasons.

3. Demonstrate how they must both verbalize why the game piece should fit in a certain season's column as well as use the clues from the pictures of the tree to explain the placement of the game pieces.

4. Inform the students that the game is won by getting pieces in the correct places in a vertical, horizontal, or diagonal row. It is important that these terms be discussed and understood.

5. Model how to play the game by gathering the students around a game board or using a transparency of the game board and pieces on the overhead. Do this modeling using a student as your partner.

6. Allow time for students to play *Season-O.*

7. As a class, close with a discussion about how a tree changes through the seasons.

8. After the game has been played several times, place two sets of laminated game pieces and a game board in a box or tub so students may continue to play the game during free time.

Discussion

1. Describe the differences in a tree through the seasons.
2. What parts of the tree seem to change a lot? Which change very little?
3. Where are the biggest changes in a tree observed?
4. Which is your favorite season of the year? Why? What does the tree look like during that time of the year?

Extension

Allow students to change the rules to the game and share their new rules with the class.

Curriculum Correlation

Language Arts

Have the class act out *My Tree, My Tree, All Year Long.*

Assessment

Have students create their own versions of *My Tree, My Tree, All Year Long.* These versions should include what is happening above, on, and below the tree during all the seasons of the year.

Home Link

Students can take the game home to play with their family by folding the game board and putting game pieces in a plastic bag.

My Tree, My Tree, All Year Long

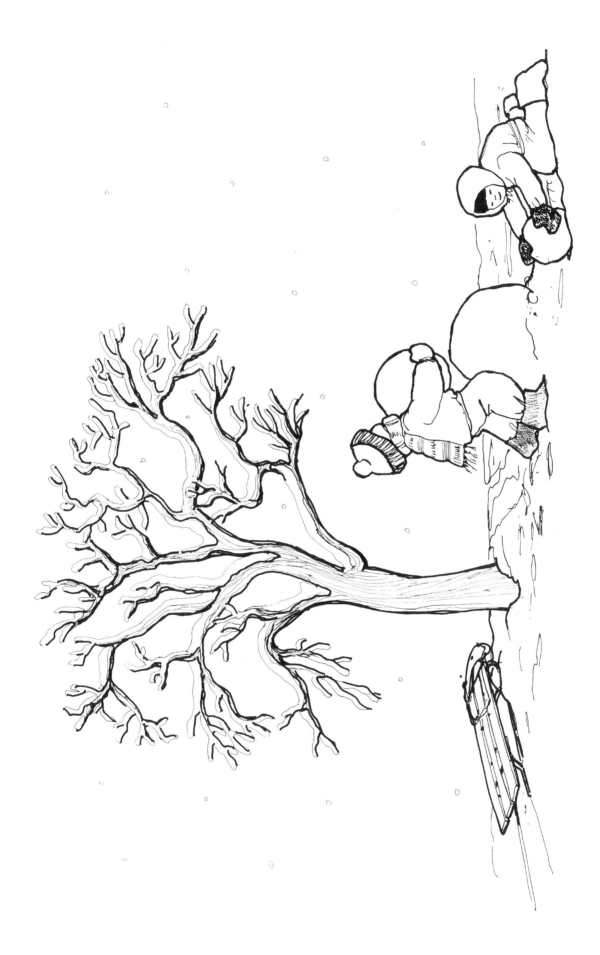

My tree bares its branches in winter;

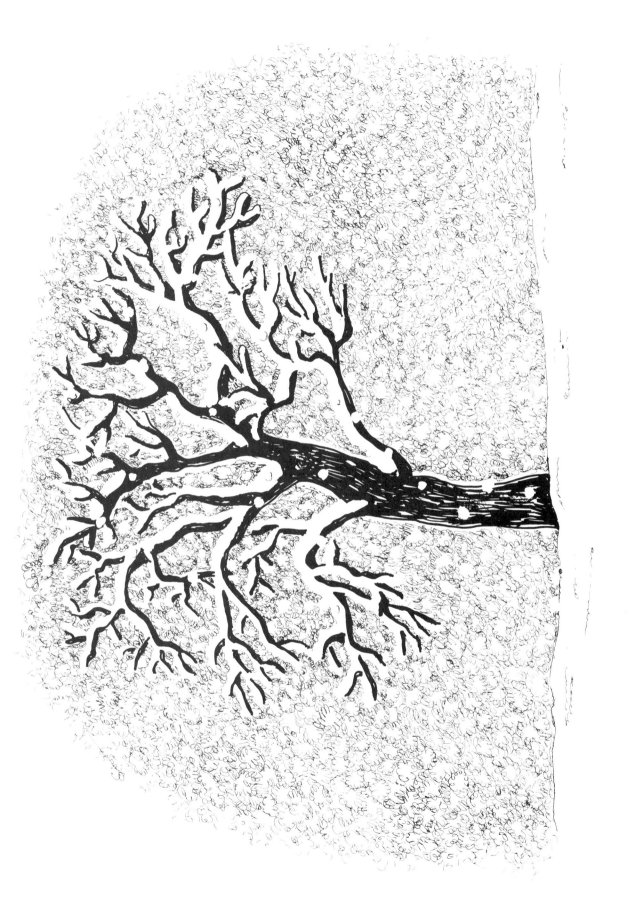

Snow on the tree,

Snow on the flowers,

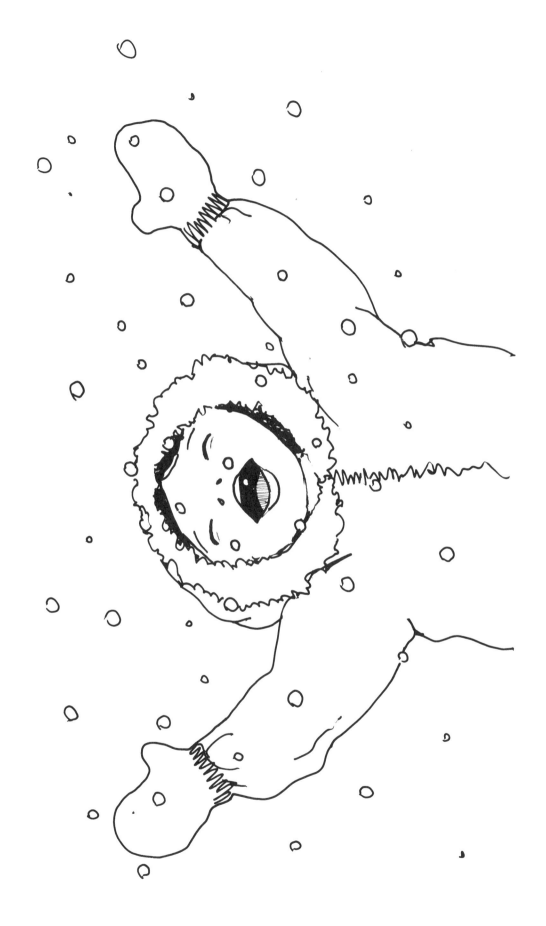

Snow on me.

My tree blooms and leafs out in springtime;

Rain on the trees,

Rain on the flowers,

Rain on me.

My tree shades and cools in summer;

Sun on the tree,

Sun on the flowers,

Sun on me.

My tree colors and drops leaves in autumn;

Wind on the tree,

Wind on the flowers,

Wind on me.

Game Board

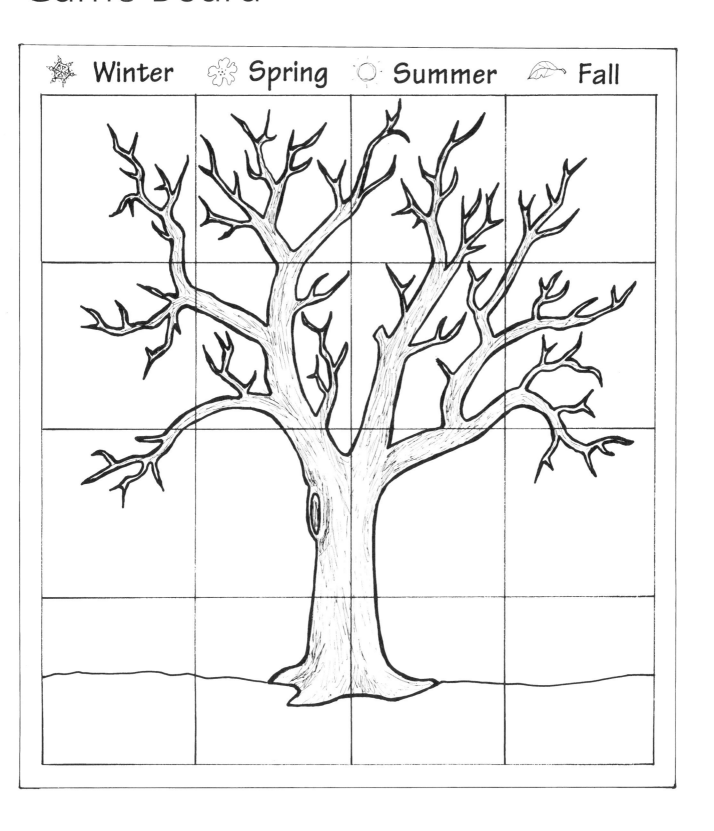

Winter   Spring   Summer   Fall

Fallen Leaf

Topic
Decomposition of leaves

Key Question
What things happen to a fallen leaf?

Focus
Students will observe the changes in leaves as they decompose.

Guiding Documents
Project 2061 Benchmarks
- *Change is something that happens to many things.*
- *Some changes are so slow or so fast they are hard to see.*
- *People can keep track of some things, seeing where they come from and where they go.*

NRC Standard
- *Plants and animals have life cycles that include being born, developing into adults, reproducing, and eventually dying. The details of the life cycle are different for different organisms.*

NCTM Standards
- *Apply estimation when working with quantities, measurement, computation, and problem solving*
- *Relate physical materials, pictures, and diagrams to mathematical ideas*
- *Collect, organize and describe data*

Math
Charting
Estimating
Counting

Science
Life science
   decomposition

Integrated Processes
Observing
Comparing and contrasting
Communicating

Collecting and recording data
Predicting
Generalizing

Materials
For each pair of students:
   2 strawberry baskets
   twist ties
   plant stakes

For the class:
   white index cards, 3" x 5"
   butcher paper, 2 meters per group of 4
   leaves

Background Information
   Young learners often experience the life cycle of plants when they plant a seed, watch it sprout, and cheer its growth. Once the plant dies, however, little attention is given to the rest of its cycle — decomposition.

   Decomposition occurs when detritus feeders (animals and protists) and decomposers (mostly fungi and bacteria) feed on dead plant and animal matter. Through this feeding, they gain nutrients for themselves and put nutrients back into the soil or water, thus forming a crucial link in the energy flow of ecosystems.

   In this activity students will observe fallen leaves as they go through nature's recycling process of decomposition. The leaves begin to decompose in different ways depending on the combination of factors which help to influence the process such as rain, freezing temperatures, wind, amount of handling, etc. Students may notice that the once supple leaves become brittle, that the veins of the leaves decompose more slowly than the membrane (this results in skeleton-looking leaves), and that the leaves break down into smaller and smaller bits.

   Eventually, the decomposed leaf becomes a part of the organically rich substance called humus. Humus provides nutrients for growing plants; thus the cycle continues.

Management
1. It is best to scout out an area that is rich with fallen leaves. If the school grounds do not provide this area, a park or vacant lot may.

2. The activity is divided into two parts: *Part 1* — observing leaf characteristics and organizing data in whole-class and group experience; *Part 2* — mini-composting in partner work.

Procedure

Part 1

1. Take the students on a walk to observe and collect fallen leaves.
2. When the students return to the classroom, have them sit in a large circle, and place several leaves in front of them.
3. Ask students what they observe about the leaves they have collected. Guide them to look at the condition of the leaves as well as size, shape, color, etc. (For example: yellow, has holes, dry, crumbly, big, round, etc.) Record their words or phrases on the white index cards. Emphasize the characteristics that indicate the leaves are decomposing.
4. Ask a student to select an index card from those with words or phrases on them. Place this card on the floor, read the word or phrase that is on it, and invite students to place the leaves that match the description around the card.
5. Ask the students to estimate how many leaves match the description, then make an actual count. Write the counted number on the card.
6. Have students pick up their leaves. Invite another student to select a different card and repeat the process until all the characteristics on the cards have been counted.
7. Ask the students to order the cards from those with the least numbers to those with the most. Have them construct number sentences from the data. (For example: "There are three more brown leaves than there are yellow leaves.") If developmentally appropriate, a Venn diagram may be used to show how some leaves fit more than one category.
8. After a thorough discussion of the data, have students collect their leaves and return to their seats to draw and write about one leaf on the first activity page.
9. Once they have completed their sketching and writing, have them fold back the picture portion of the activity sheet so that only the description of the leaf shows. Divide the students into groups of eight and have them place the leaves in the center of their newly formed group. Direct them to read their descriptions one at a time and see if the others in their group can determine which leaf is being described.

Part 2

1. If possible, set up a large compost heap outside the classroom. This can be done by raking leaves together in a pile and placing some wire around the leaves to keep them from blowing away. Water can be added to accelerate the decomposition process as well as to keep the leaves from blowing away. This compost heap can be used for making comparisons with students' mini-compost heaps.
2. Inform students that they will be building their own miniature compost heaps by attaching one strawberry basket to the ground with plant stakes. Direct them to use the leaves they collected in *Part 1* and layer them in the basket. Then have them use another strawberry basket as a lid. Use twist ties to secure the lid to the bottom basket. (Do not add water or soil.)

3. Copy as many student pages of the basket and paper as necessary. Over the course of the next two weeks, allow time for students to record the changes in the leaves in their miniature compost heap. Encourage them to smell and touch (they may observe some warmth), as well as look at the leaves. Have them make sketches to show the changes they observe (level changes as well as color changes) and describe their sensory observations. Suggest to them that they indicate and record the depth of the leaves in the basket by counting the number of basket grids.
4. After a few weeks, have students add a little water to their mini-compost heap and observe the changes.
5. Continue this process for at least a month.

Discussion

1. What does *decomposition* mean to you?
2. What are some characteristics of decomposing leaves?
3. Did all leaves decompose at the same rate? Explain.
4. What happened to the decomposing leaves (size, color, texture)?
5. What conditions seemed to make the leaves decompose faster?
6. Tell how a newly fallen leaf and a decomposed leaf are alike. How are they different?
7. What happens to a leaf after it decomposes? [It becomes a part of the soil and it helps feed new plants.]
8. What other tests would you like to perform on your leaves?

Extensions

1. Look at various types of soil with a hand lens or microscope to see if you can find parts of leaves that are decomposing.
2. Interview people to find out how they take care of fallen leaves.
3. Plant some seeds in soil that has been enriched with decomposed leaves for the students' outdoor compost heap. Compare the growth of these plants with plants growing in non-enriched soil.
4. Locate someone who has a compost pile. Ask that person to speak to the students about the upkeep and use of compost. Or take a field trip to the composter's yard or garden to observe the compost being used.
5. Have students investigate various conditions that may increase the rate of decomposition in mini-compost heap. Some suggestions are:
   - adding water
   - covering with dirt
   - putting in freezing temperatures (use a freezer)
   - adding table scraps such as potato or apple peels.

   Two optional student pages have been included to record the observations. Have students cut along the broken lines and staple the pages together to make booklets.

Curriculum Correlation
Literature

Lavies, Bianca. *Compost Critter*. Dutton Children's Books. New York. 1993.

Markle, Sandra. *Outside and Inside Trees*. Bradbury Press. New York. 1993.

Tresselt, Alvin. *The Gift of the Tree*. Lothrop, Lee and Shepard Books. New York. 1992.

Home Link

Encourage families to build a compost heap and use it in their gardens or flower beds.

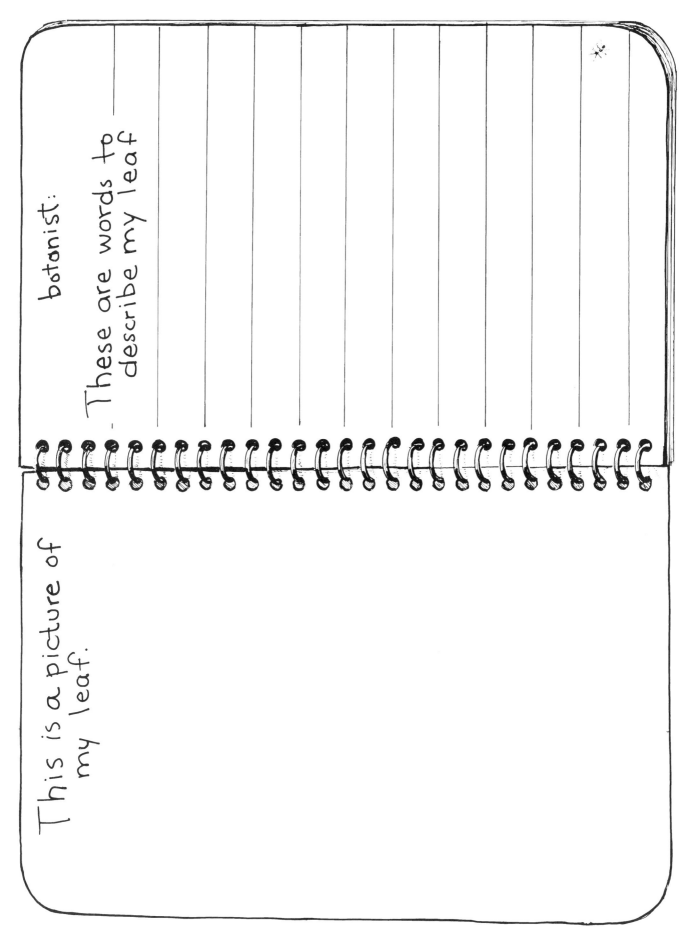

botanist:

These are words to
describe my leaf

This is a picture of
my leaf.

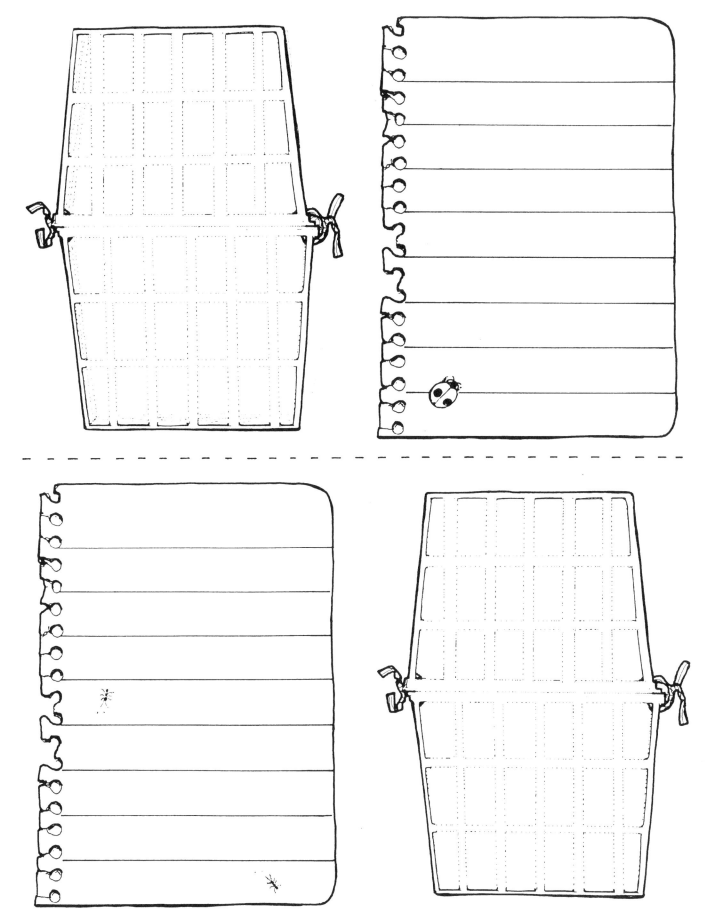

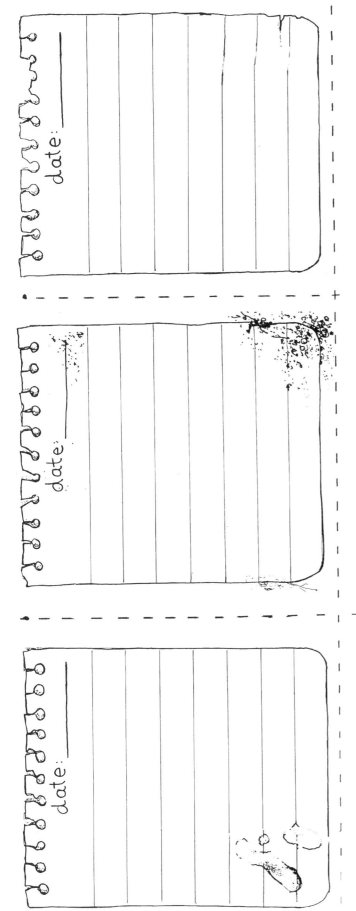

date: _____

date: _____

date: _____

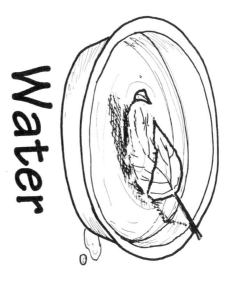

Water

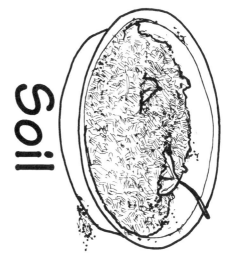

Soil

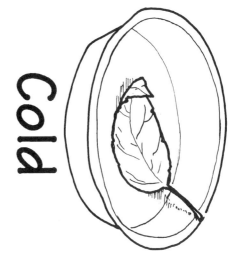

Cold

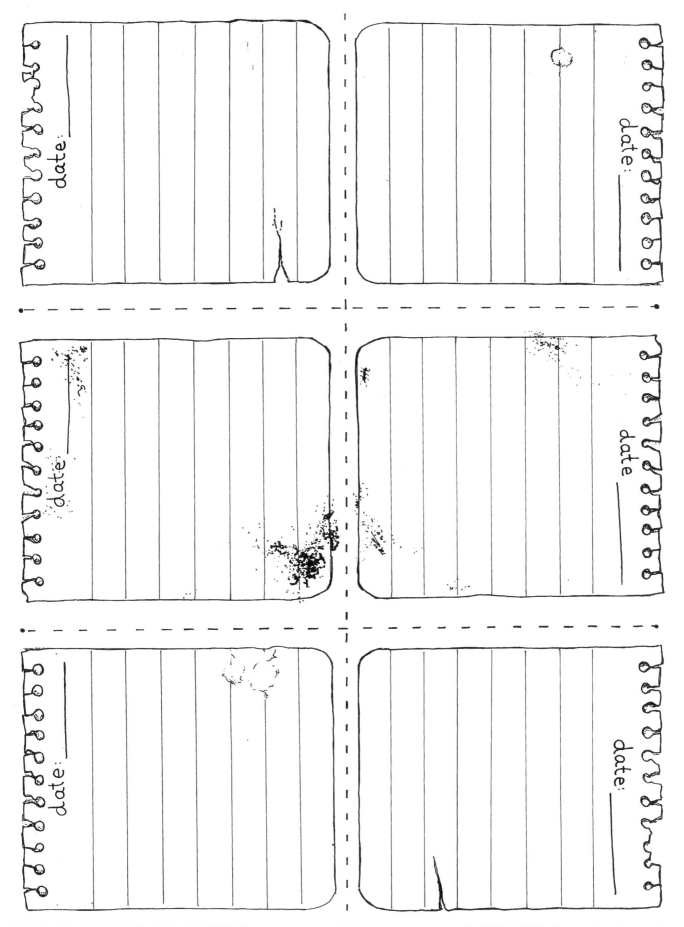

date: _____

date _____

date: _____

date _____

date: _____

date: _____

Dirt Baggers

Topic
Soil contents: living, once living and non-living

Key Questions
1. What kind of materials do you find in soil?
2. Which of these materials are living? ...once living? ... non-living?

Focus
Students will learn about the diverse materials in soil by sorting it. They will then examine their sorting again to determine if the found materials are living, once living, or non-living.

Guiding Documents
Project 2061 Benchmarks
- *Change is something that happens to many things.*
- *Animals and plants sometimes cause changes in their surroundings.*

NRC Standards
- *Earth materials are solid rocks and soils, water and the gases of the atmosphere. The varied materials have different physical and chemical properties, which make them useful in different ways, for example, as building materials, as sources of fuel, or for growing the plants we use as food. Earth materials provide many of the resources that humans use.*
- *Soils have properties of color and texture, capacity to retain water, and ability to support the growth of many kinds of plants, including those in our food supply.*

NCTM Standard
- *Collect, organize and describe data*

Math
Graphing
Sorting

Science
Earth science
    soil

Integrated Processes
Observing
Comparing and contrasting
Communicating
Collecting and recording data

Materials
For the class:
    4 sheets of chart paper
    4 glue sticks
For each group:
    4 index cards, 3" x 5"
    1 quart bag filled with soil sample
    10 snack-size plastic bags with zipper seal
    hand lens
    newspapers
    sorting tools such as strainer, tweezers, toothpicks
    3 paper plates
    glue

Background Information
On much of the land surface of the Earth lies a relatively thin layer of loose material called *soil*. It can be a few inches deep or it can extend down several feet.

The word *soil* comes from the Latin word *solum*, which means *floor* or *ground*. Soil is the ground or foundation of all life on land. It supports the plants and animals on which humans and all other living things depend.

Soil is a mixture of organic and inorganic materials. The *texture* or *feel* of soil depends on the particle size and the relative amounts of organic and inorganic materials in it.

Inorganic materials are made up of particles of rocks and minerals, substances which were not formed from living things. Most inorganic soils are a mixture of coarse to fine particles classified as sand, silt, and clay.

Organic materials consist of living things and the remains of once living things. *Humus* is the decaying organic matter which adds nutrients to the soil and helps to separate the tightly packed inorganic materials, allowing the soil to receive and hold more air and water than it would otherwise hold. Humus provides food for bacteria and other microorganisms which break down dead organic matter, forming substances plants can use.

The soil contains many living things which help the soil in some way. Plant roots grow down into the soil, holding it, and helping to prevent it from being blown or washed away. Many animals such as mice, squirrels, and moles make their burrows there. Their holes and tunnels let still more air and water into the soil. Animals such as beetles, ants, slugs, earthworms, and spiders feed on and excrete organic matter, thus facilitating the process of decay and soil formation.

Management

1. This activity should be done in small groups.
2. Collect the soil ahead of time. It should contain some of these materials: rocks, sticks, leaves, seeds, roots, insects, worms, pine needles, and sand or clay. If the soil does not contain a good sampling of these materials, you may wish to add some to the samples.
3. Cover the tables with newspaper before doing this activity.
4. Have students use an index card on which to draw any living things found in the soil and then they may release them outside in the area where the soil sample was collected.
5. Select an area where the class graphs can be seen by all students.
6. Check your samples and make any additional, related category labels needed for items in soil that are found. An example might be a *living* sow bug and a *dead* one.
7. Tape and mark three pieces of chart paper together to create an eight column graph. This will be used in *Part 1*. Divide the remaining piece of paper into three sections and label the sections: living, non-living, once living.

Procedure

Part 1: Sorting the materials in the soil

1. Hold up a bag of soil and ask the students what they think they might find in the soil if they were to sort it carefully.
2. After developing a list of predicted materials on the board, distribute a bag of soil and sorting tools to each group.
3. Allow each group time to sort their soil using the sorting tools. They should make piles of each found material on the newspaper cover.
4. Guide students to share their findings with the class.
5. Ask them if they think their sample had the same materials and amounts as the other groups.
6. To determine what materials each group found, ask them to cut paper plates into fourths and glue a sample of each material on a piece of the plate.
7. Begin by holding up each label and asking who found material in their soil like the label. If a group did, invite a representative to bring up the paper plate wedge and use a glue stick to adhere it to the graph above the label. Continue the

process until all labels have been used. Provide for the other materials the students have sorted by using the blank labels.
8. Have them place the rest of their sorted materials in bags and put the bags on extra paper plates for use in *Part 2*. Direct each student to write their name on the plate to identify the group.

Part 2: Determining which materials are living, once living, and non-living

1. Direct the students' attention to the soil sample graph they made. Ask them how they would describe the materials found. If they do not bring up the fact that some items are living, some once living, and some never living, it may be necessary for you to talk about that grouping.
2. Ask them questions about perplexing items such as seeds, an earwig's wing, shells, a piece of granite, etc.
3. Once you have determined that the students understand the labels on the three column chart, have them sort their soil samples into living, once living, and non-living catergories. (*Living* items should be illustrated on the index cards.)
4. Direct them to cut the remaining paper plates in fourths and sprinkle a small amount of each material (or picture) they found on a section of paper plate, using a new section for each material.
5. Tell groups to determine where the materials should be placed on the chart labeled *living, once living,* and *non-living.* Allow them time to decide and then have them send a representative up with their samples. Have them glue the samples on the class graph in the proper column.
6. Ask the students to look at the graph and come up with three statements about it as a group.
7. Allow them time to share their group statements.
8. Let student go back to the sorted materials and combine them again. Have them make three small bags of their samples, two to trade with other groups. After they have traded for two other samples, have them staple the samples to the activity sheet provided.
9. Have students use the recording page to write statements about their three soil samples.

Discussion

1. What materials did we find in the soil?
2. Describe material that is living. ... was living. ... was never living.
3. What did you observe about particles of sand and/or clay?
4. Did you find any materials that surprised your group?
5. If you looked in your backyard, what do you think your soil would look like?

Extensions

1. Have students place a magnet in a plastic bag and run it through the soil sample to determine if any magnetic materials are present.
2. Allow students to plant seeds in the various samples of soil and compare the growth rates.
3. Have each group put a small amount of their soil sample in a jar partially filled with water. Tell them to shake the jar and then observe what happens: after two minutes, ten minutes, and 24 hours. (Once living material will usually float to the surface.)

Home Link

Students should take their soil samples home and share them with their family by describing the materials. They could bring a sample of their home soil back to school to compare it with the class samples.

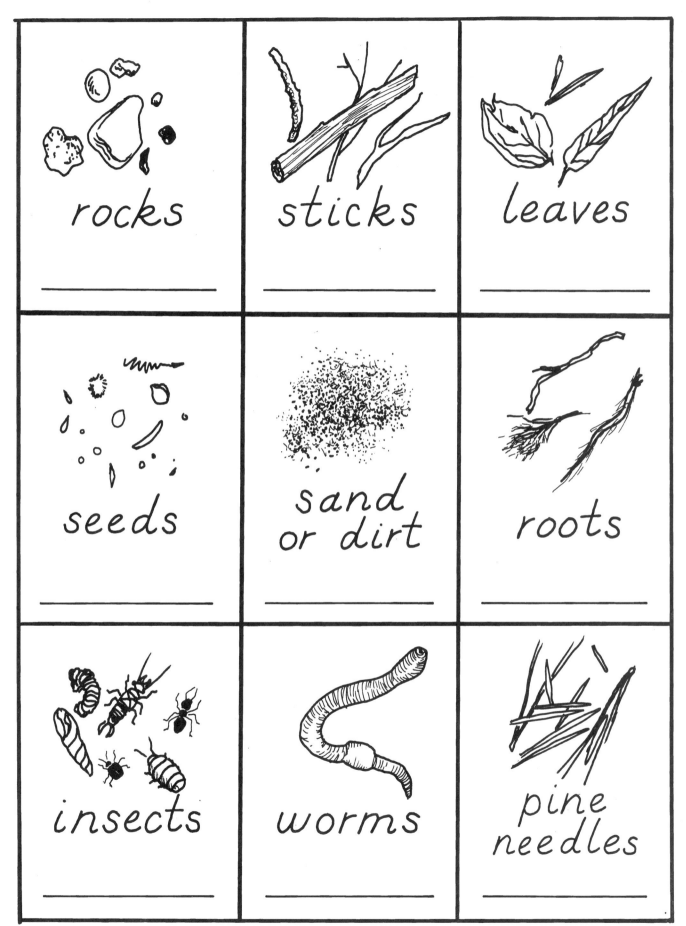

rocks

sticks

leaves

seeds

sand or dirt

roots

insects

worms

pine needles

Staple sample 3 here.

Staple sample 2 here.

Staple sample 1 here.

D
I
R
T

B
A
G
G
E
R
S

Dirt Bagger

DIRT BAGGERS

Dirt Bagger _____

Sky Watchers

Topic
Changes in the sky

Key Question
What can we observe in the sky and how does it change?

Focus
Students will become sky watchers by observing the day and night skies.

Guiding Documents
Project 2061 Benchmarks
- *Some events in nature have a repeating pattern. The weather changes some from day to day, but things such as temperature and rain (or snow) tend to be high, low, or medium in the same months every year.*
- *The sun can be seen only in the daytime, but the moon can be seen sometimes at night and sometimes during the day. The sun, moon and stars all appear to move slowly across the sky.*

NRC Standards
- *The sun, moon, stars, clouds, birds, and airplanes all have properties, locations, and movements that can be observed and described.*
- *Objects in the sky have patterns of movement. The sun, for example, appears to move across the sky in the same way every day, but its path changes slowly over the seasons. The moon moves across the sky on a daily basis much like the sun. The observable shape of the moon changes from day to day in a cycle that lasts about a month.*

NCTM Standard
- *Relate physical materials, pictures and diagrams to mathematical ideas*

Science
Earth science
   day and night

Integrated Processes
Observing
Contrasting and comparing
Communicating
Applying
Predicting

Materials
For the class:
   chart paper
   blue and gray paper (see *Management 4*)

Background Information
"It is daytime, I can play outside now. It is night and dark. I am afraid of the dark." Students use day and night as criteria for determining what they can and cannot do. Before children learn that the rotation of the Earth on its axis causes day and night, they first need to observe day and night as a pattern that repeats on a regular basis. This understanding lays the groundwork for future understandings of the rotations and revolutions of our Earth's system.

Management
1. Since much of this activity is based on outdoor observation, you may wish to time your investigations for a period just before or after recess.
2. *Part 1*, which is done on the first day of this activity, is merely observation both during the day and at night. *Part 2*, done on the second day, has students record their own observations in a circle book for two days at school and then they take the book home the next two nights to observe the night sky.
3. The amount of time needed for outside observations is dependent on how many things can be seen in the sky. The maximum amount of time would probably be 15 minutes.
4. Copy the day portions of the book on blue paper and the night on gray paper.

Procedure
Part 1
1. Read Gail Gibbons' book *Sun Up, Sun Down,* or one of the other books suggested in *Curriculum Correlation*. Ask students what they think they will see in the sky when they go out to recess. Record their predictions on a piece of chart paper.
2. After recess point to the predictions written on the board and discuss what they actually saw in the sky. When students describe what they saw, ask them to also indicate where they saw the object and add this information to the chart.
3. Before going to lunch, tell them they should observe the sky again during lunch recess. Ask them if they think they will still see any of the things

they saw before? If they indicate they will, ask them if they think those things will have changed in any way. Discuss any new item they think they might see. Direct the students to do their observation some time during lunch time.

4. When students return from lunch, have them share what they observed. Record their observations on the chart paper.

5. Optional: This may also be done at the afternoon recess.

6. Just before going home, ask the students what they might see in the night sky and record their predictions. Read *Switch On The Night* by Ray Bradbury.

7. When students return to school the next day, ask them what they saw in the night sky. Record their observations on the chart and compare these observations to the predictions they made.

Part 2

1. Show students how to construct the circle book and then have them make their own, writing their name on the cover.

2. Before going outside to observe, demonstrate how to sit with a partner, back-to-back style, so they can observe the sky and also have
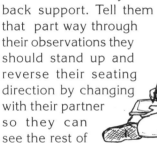
back support. Tell them that part way through their observations they should stand up and reverse their seating direction by changing with their partner so they can see the rest of
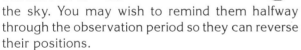
the sky. You may wish to remind them halfway through the observation period so they can reverse their positions.

3. Tell them that while outside, they will do quick pencil sketches on a piece of scratch paper, but they will make more detailed drawings of their observations in their circle book when they return to the room.

4. Once the students have returned to the classroom, allow them time to transfer their sketched ideas to the day portion of the book (first blue section). Ask students to share what they saw.

5. Repeat the procedure later in the day and have them make notes as to anything that has changed.

6. On the following day, have students again make and record observations.

7. Before it is time to go home on this day, show the students the two gray parts of their book and tell them this is where they will record their observations of the night sky for the next two nights. Record their predictions of what they think will see tonight and the following night.

8. Read the *Parent Letter* to the students and then send it and the circle book home with the them.

9. After students have observed the sky for two nights, have them share their nighttime observations and book.

Discussion

1. How are the things in the sky the same each day? ... different?

2. Were there things you observed in the sky that surprised you? Explain.

3. What are the similarities in the day and night sky? What are the differences?

4. If you reversed the procedure and looked at the day sky at home or the night sky at school, how might they be the same? ... different?

5. Did you enjoy looking at the sky?

6. Explain why day or night is your favorite.

Extension

Continue observing the sky and keeping a Sky Watchers journal.

Curriculum Correlation

Literature:

Bradbury, Ray. *Switch On The Night.* Alfred A. Knopf. New York. 1955.

Fowler, Allan. *The Sun Is Always Shining Somewhere.* Children's Press. Chicago. 1991.

Gibbons, Gail. *Sun Up, Sun Down.* Harcourt Brace Jovanovich. San Diego. 1983.

Marzollo, Jean. *Sun Song.* HarperCollins Publisher. New York. 1995.

Home Link

Families should participate in the night sky observation following the directions in the family letter.

In Appreciation

The idea for the circle book format comes from Dinah Zike's *Big Book of Book and Activities*. Many other ideas may be gained by accessing this book from: Dinah-Might Activities, Inc. P.O. Box 39657, San Antonio, Texas 78218, (512)657-5951.

Directions For Sky Watching Book

1. Copy the circle onto blue and gray paper. Each student will need two blues (day) and two grays (night).

2. Have them carefully cut out each circle.

3. Direct them to fold each circle in half along the solid line with words on the outside of the fold.

 4. Then have them fold each circle in half again forming fourths. The words are folded to the inside of the fourths.

5. Have them glue each folded circle to another, alternately stacking blue and gray colors — day to night, day to night. Make sure that the folded edges match. When all circles have been stacked on each other  and glued, direct students to unfold the "wing" of the bottom circle to make it a half circle and the top circle "wing" to make it a half. Have students then glue the two "wings" that now overlap.

6. For each observation, have them write their name, date, and time of observation and then write what they see. To draw an illustration of the day or night sky, direct them to open a circle and drag on the complete circle.

7. This book may be hung as a mobile which will show all the illustrations.

113

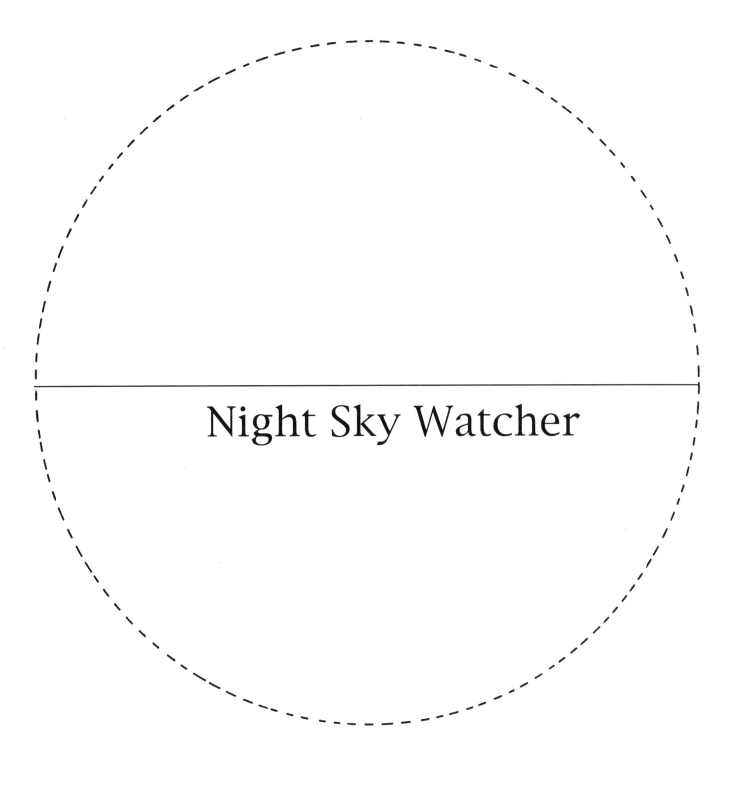

Night Sky Watcher

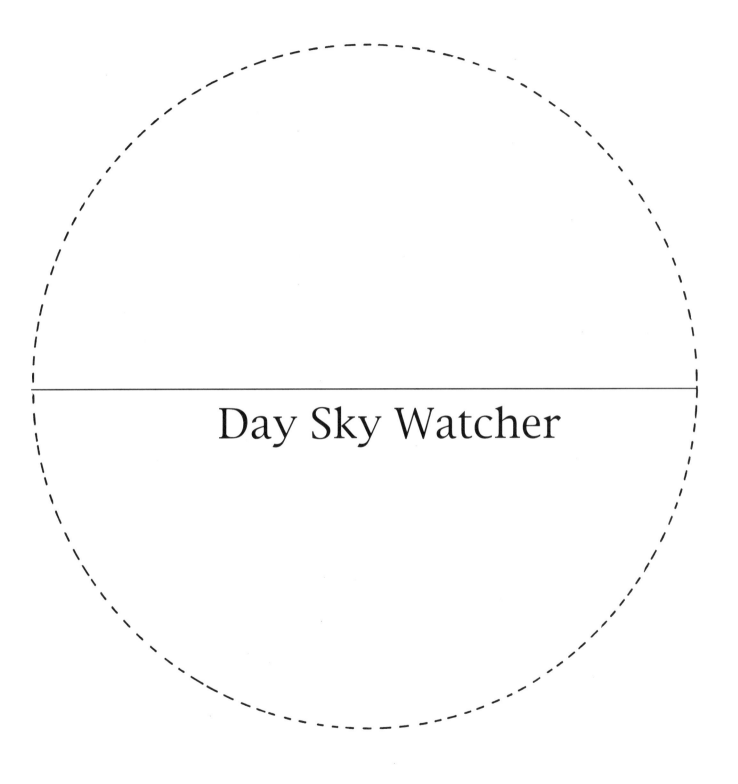

Day Sky Watcher

Dear Families,

Our class is learning about how the sky changes and about day and night. Please help your child to carefully observe the night sky for the next two evenings. Help him or her to look at the sky and record all the objects that can be seen. A pair of binoculars, if available, will add another dimension to the observational experience.

Your child should record on a gray circle of their book what he or she sees each night. You can help your child write about the night sky.

Please return these books after you and your child have observed the sky for two nights.

Happy Observing!

Mr. Groundhog, Mr. Groundhog

Topic
Light and shadows

Key Questions
1. Will we see Mr. Groundhog's shadow?
2. What will happen to Mr. Groundhog's shadow as we observe it during the day?

Focus
Students will observe, trace, and discuss the shadow of a groundhog throughout a day.

Guiding Documents
Project 2061 Benchmarks
- *Like all planets and stars, the earth is approximately spherical in shape. The rotation of the earth on its axis every 24 hours produces the night-and-day cycle. To people on earth, this turning of the planet makes it seem as though the sun, moon, planets, and stars are orbiting the earth once a day.*
- *Keep records of their investigations and observations and not change the records later.*

NRC Standards
- *The position of an object can be described by locating it relative to another object or the background.*
- *An object's motion can be described by tracing and measuring its position over time.*
- *The sun, moon, stars, clouds, birds, and airplanes all have properties, locations, and movements that can be observed and described.*

NCTM Standard
- *Relate physical materials, pictures, and diagrams to mathematical ideas*

Math
Measurement

Science
Physical science
   Earth's rotation
      shadows

Integrated Processes
Observing
Comparing and contrasting
Communicating
Collecting and recording data
Interpreting data

Materials
For the class:
   Mr. *Groundhog* pattern (see *Management 1*)
   stick with pointed end, 30 inches long
   hammer
   large sheet of butcher paper (see *Management 2*)
   five markers of different colors

Background Information
Young learners usually experience shadows in relation to themselves. "My shadow keeps following me." "My shadow sure is getting tall and skinny." These observations, along with reflective discussions about them, form a very important foundation for later understandings. These prior observations are essential for students to eventually develop understandings about the relationship of the angle of the sun at different times of the day and the resulting change in an object's shadow. Many young learners do observe that the sun's position seems to change, as does their own shadow and the shadows of other objects (such as Mr. Groundhog in this activity). It is quite a leap, however, to assume that they make the connection in the observed changes in a shadow and the relative position of the Earth and sun.

We as teachers of young children need to have a greater understanding of what causes the changes in the shadows students are observing. It helps us ask appropriate questions that will direct children to reflect about the changes they are seeing. At this age level, the focus is on the observation of a shadow's change rather than the "why" of the change.

It is important for us as adults to know that shadows are created as objects block the sun's rays. The changes in shadows occur because the Earth rotates on its axis in a counterclockwise motion causing the sun to be seen in the eastern sky in the morning and in the western sky in the evening. Shadows that are cast because of the sun's apparent motion can be marked and measured. As the Earth rotates, the angle of the sun's rays on an object changes. As the angle of the sun changes in relation to the object blocking its light, the shadow of that object will change in length, width, and position.

Early in the morning, when the sun is low on the horizon, the resulting shadow is relatively long, thin, and located to the west of the object. As the day progresses, when the sun seems to move higher in the sky, the shadow gets shorter and plumper. When the sun is nearly overhead, the shadow will be at its shortest. Later in the day, the sun's relative position causes the shadow to lengthen again, but it now appears on the other side (east) of the object. Other changes in the shadow's position and length will occur with seasonal changes.

Management

1. The groundhog figure is constructed by making a transparency of the picture provided. Place it on the overhead projector and then move the projector until the projected image is approximately 24 inches tall and 15 inches wide. Cut a piece of brown butcher paper twice the length and width of the groundhog. Fold the paper in half and trace the groundhog shape onto the double thickness. Cut the doubled paper. Staple the two layers all around the groundhog's body, leaving the bottom open. Stuff the the groundhog's body with newspaper, then staple the bottom closed.
2. Create a mat on which to trace the groundhog's shadow by taping side-by-side two five-foot lengths of butcher paper.
3. Look for an area outside where shadows from buildings, trees, or poles will not interfer with the groundhog's shadow. It must also be an area where the class can form a circle and be seated around Mr. Groundhog and the tracing mat.
4. Hammer the stake into the ground in the center of the mat. Insert the stake up through the bottom part of Mr. Groundhog's body.
5. If wind is a problem, either put heavy objects on each end of the mat or use plant stakes around the edges to keep the wind from moving the mat.
6. Make sure to use a different color each time you trace the groundhog's shadow. It is difficult to trace so the teacher may need to do the tracing.
7. If you wish to do the shadow prediction part of the activity, you will need to make a graph by enlarging the one provided. Prediction markers are included.

Procedure

1. Read one of the stories suggested in *Curriculum Correlation* about groundhogs and shadows. Ask the students if the groundhog would see its shadow today. If desired, the students can use the prediction markers provided on the enlarged chart. Discuss the predictions before going outside to check.
2. Take the students outside and have them form a circle around the groundhog and the tracing mat. Ask about the shadow and discuss their observations. Trace the groundhog's shadow as the students watch. Ask students what time it is and record the time inside the traced shadow. Also inside the shadow outline, record some of their observations about the shadow.

Ask students what they just did at school before coming out to see the shadow. Record their responses inside the traced shadow. (For example: 8:30 A.M. The groundhog's shadow is longer than the groundhog is tall. We just had calendar time.)
3. Wait about an hour and ask the children what they think Mr. Groundhog's shadow will look like now. After students make their predictions, go out again and make a circle around Mr. Groundhog and the tracing mat. They should discuss what they observe. Trace the groundhog's shadow and inside record the time of observation, what changes they have observed in the shadow, and what they have just done before coming outside. (For example: 10:00 A.M. Mr. Groundhog is shrinking. He is getting skinnier. We just finished snack.)
4. Repeat this process as many times as possible, each time observing the students and noting their observation skills.
5. Ask the students to describe how the groundhog's shadow changed.
6. Ask them what changes might happen to their shadows during the day.
7. If possible, repeat this experience several times during the year.

Discussion

1. What causes a shadow?
2. Describe how Mr. Groundhog's shadow changed.
3. What changes did you observe?
4. Tell about your own shadow.
5. Explain how the game of shadow tag might change if you played it in the morning and then at lunch.
6. What did you learn by doing this activity?

Assessment

A few days after this activity, ask students to trace their own shadow in the early morning. After they have traced their shadow, ask them to think about Mr. Groundhog and then explain how their shadows will change. This can be done in writing or by having students dictate their predictions to you if they are not yet fluent writers.

Extensions

Students can observe, trace, and discuss the changes in the shadow of the sunflower, scarecrow, or other figures at different times of the year.

Curriculum Correlation

Kroll, Steven. *It's Groundhog Day.* Scholastic, Inc. New York. 1987.

Tompert, Ann. *Nothing Sticks Like A Shadow.* Houghton Mifflin Co. Boston. 1984.

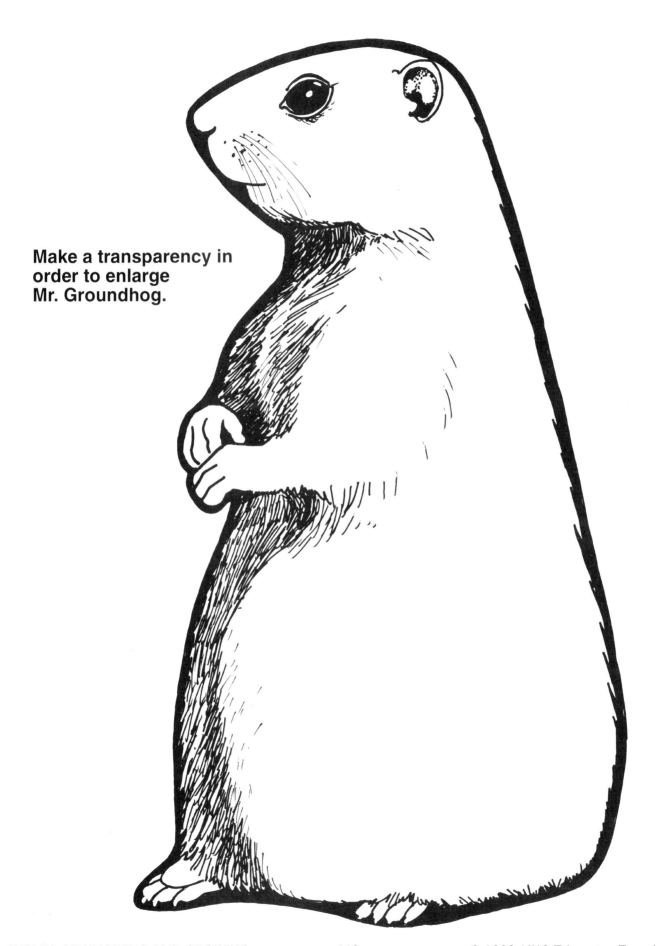

Make a transparency in order to enlarge Mr. Groundhog.

WILL THE GROUNDHOG SEE ITS SHADOW?

YES

NO

Prediction Markers

Look at the Moon

Topic
Moon cycle

Key Question
How can we describe the changes we see in the moon?

Focus
Students will observe the sky over a period of months to determine how the moon changes.

Guiding Documents
Project 2061 Benchmarks
- *The sun can be seen only in the daytime, but the moon can be seen sometimes at night and sometimes during the day. The sun, moon and stars all apear to move slowly across the sky.*
- *The moon looks a little different every day, but looks the same again about every four weeks.*

NRC Standards
- *The sun, moon, stars, clouds, birds and airplanes all have properties, movements and locations that can be observed and described.*
- *Objects in the sky have patterns of movement. The sun, for example, appears to move across the sky in the same way every day, but its path changes slowly over the seasons. The moon moves across the sky on daily basis much like the sun. The observable shape of the moon changes from day to day in a cycle that lasts about a month.*

NCTM Standards
- *Investigate and predict the results of combining, subdividing, and changing shapes*
- *Recognize and appreciate geometry in their world*
- *Construct, read, and interpret displays of data*

Math
Geometric shapes
Patterns

Science
Earth science
    phases of the moon

Integrated Processes
Observing
Comparing and contrasting
Communicating
Collecting and recording data
Organizing data
Predicting

Materials
For the class:
    calendar or chart to record daily observations
    butcher paper

For each student:
    1-meter strip of adding machine paper
    clothespin
    3" x 5" index card

Background Information
After observing the night sky for several months, young learners should understand that the moon changes in a predictable pattern. They should be able to describe the observable shapes of the moon (crescent, quarter, half, full, new). It is doubtful that they will understand that the moon waxes, (gets larger) on its right side and wanes (gets smaller) on its left side, or that the waxing sequence builds from the new moon phase to the full moon phase and the waning sequence follows the full moon phase diminishing to the new moon phase.

Young learners are not ready for the reasoning of why there are phases of the moon. However, we, as their teachers, need to know that the moon's phases are determined by the position of the moon in relation to the Earth and the sun.

When the moon is between the Earth and sun, we cannot see the lighted face and therefore we see a new (dark) moon. As the moon continues in its orbit around the Earth, the small part of it that we see reflects the sun's light and we see a sliver, or crescent moon. When the moon forms a right angle (90 degrees) with the Earth and sun, we see the first quarter. As the moon continues its orbit around the Earth, the moon continues to wax (grow) creating an enlarged D-shape called the gibbous phase. When it is in the opposite side of the Earth from the sun, we see a full moon. The moon then begins its waning phases (getting smaller), moving through the waning gibbous, quarter, waning crescent to new moon.

The moon can be seen at different times of day and night. The full moon is above the horizon from sunset to sunrise, the first quarter is observable from noon to midnight, and the third quarter from midnight to noon.

Enjoy the magic of watching the moon and night sky and encourage students to do the same. The enjoyment of watching the rhythms of the sky will become infectious and entire families will join in.

Management
1. It is best to observe the moon over a period of three months if students are to really understand the cyclical process of the phases of the moon.
2. Provide an enlarged calendar or chart to record the daily discussions of the prior night's observations.
3. A few minutes each day will be important and needed for discussions and observations to be shared. This can be done in opening or closing of the day.
4. The teacher should write a letter to the families so they understand how to support their children and actually participate in the observations of the moon's cycle.

5. Copy the *Moon on a Strip* on tagboard so it will be sturdy enough to hold a clothespin.
6. Observations are greatly enhanced by using binoculars.

Procedure
1. Ask the students to draw a picture of the moon on an index card. Direct them to place these cards in the chalk tray, on the bulletin board, or in some other place where everyone can look at the pictures. Discuss how the pictures are alike and how they are different. If students mainly draw the full moon, ask if there are other shapes of the moon not represented.
2. Hold up a piece of butcher paper and ask the students if there is a way to organize the pictures on this paper. Allow time for discussion of how to organize them. Some suggestions might be: all similar phases together, all phases half to full together, favorite phases. Decide on which suggestion to use and construct a chart or graph.
3. After discussing the arrangements, ask the students how the moon changes (*Key Question*). Record these statements below the chart or graph.
4. On a piece of adding machine paper which has been folded into 5 cm (2") segments, have students predict how the moon seems to change.
5. Show them the *Moon Observation Calendar* and explain how they will be drawing what they observe about the moon's shape in each date's box. Tell them they should observe carefully and record what they see.
6. Send the *Moon Observation Calendar* home with a letter to the families.
7. Each day record the students' observations (for example: shape, features, size, position, time, and place observed) and allow time for comparisons and discussion. Record the moon phase on the class calendar.
8. Encourage students to continue to observe the moon each night as well as record the shape of the moon. Allow time for them to share their observations with the class the next day. Students can also keep a written observation in the *Moon Observation Journal*.
9. At the beginning of the next month, discuss how the moon changed over the past month. Ask them to predict the pattern of the moon for the next month. Have them revise their former adding machine paper predictions.
10. Give each student the activity sheet with the *Moon on a Strip*. Direct them to tape or glue the strips together and then write the date their new moon observation will begin and have them sequentially number the other dates.
11. Have them take their *Moon Observation Journal* home and each night record what they observe. The next morning, direct them to record what they observed on the *Moon Observation Strip* which they have left folded in their desk at school.
12. Continue recording students' observations of how the moon seems to change on the class calendar.
13. When this second month's observation is completed, give the students a clothespin. They should write "Last Night" on the blade of the clothespin.
14. For the next month, have them move the clothespin along the *Month on a Strip* according to the changes they observe each night and discuss how the changes follow a very predictable pattern.
15. To culminate this experience, read the included book *Look at the Moon*.

Discussion
1. How does the moon change?
2. Were there nights you could not see the moon? Why?
3. How would you describe the shapes of the moon to someone?
4. What were the times you saw the moon?
5. Where would you recommend someone go in your yard to see the moon?
6. What was your favorite shape of the moon?
7. Why is it important to know about the moon cycle?

Extensions
1. Make a model of the phases of the moon using two different colors of clay.
2. Have a night sky observation party and invite an amateur astronomer to bring a telescope to aid in making observations. The students can also look at the moon through binoculars.
3. Have students bring in various calendars from home and share how they represent the cycle of the moon.

Curriculum Correlation
Language Arts
   Branley, Franklyn M. *The Moon Seems to Change.* HarperCollins Publishers. New York. 1987.
   Willard, Nancy. *Nightgown of the Sullen Moon.* Harcourt Brace Jovanovich. Orlando, FL. 1983.

Art
   Make a circle by tracing around a large circular object with yellow crayon. Decide which is your favorite phase of the moon and shade that part by pressing hard on the yellow crayon. With a blue wash (tempera paint watered down to wash consistency), paint over the moon shape. Write or tell why this is your favorite phase of the moon.

Home Link
   The nightly moon observation and calendar recording should be a family project.

Assessment
   Have students return to their predictions made on adding machine paper in the first part of the activity. Using a new strip of paper, ask them to record what they now know about how the moon seems to change.

date | date | date | date

date | date | date | date

Moon on a Strip

by:

Astronomer's Name

date | date | date | date

date | date | date | date | date

date | date | date | date | date

date | date | date | date | date

date | date | date | date | date

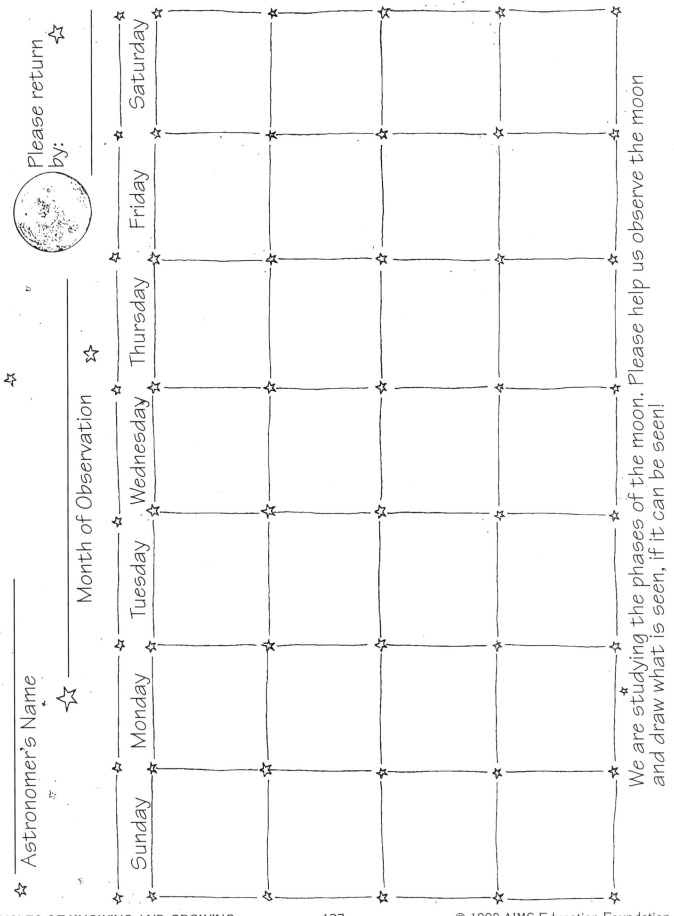

Astronomer's Name _____

Month of Observation _____

Please return by: _____

Sunday	Monday	Tuesday	Wednesday	Thursday	Friday	Saturday

We are studying the phases of the moon. Please help us observe the moon and draw what is seen, if it can be seen!

128

☆ Date_____ Time_____

Place_____

Words to describe the moon.

_____

_____

_____

_____

_____

My drawing of
the moon

- -

✂

_____

_____

_____

_____

_____

Words to describe the moon.

My drawing of
the moon

Place_____

Date_____ Time_____

Look at the Moon

by Barbara Ann Novelli

Look at the moon tonight, tell us what you see.

Is the moon tonight a half?

Does it shine a silver D?

Look at the moon again.
Does it form a big round ball?

We call this moon a full moon.

It dances on the wall.

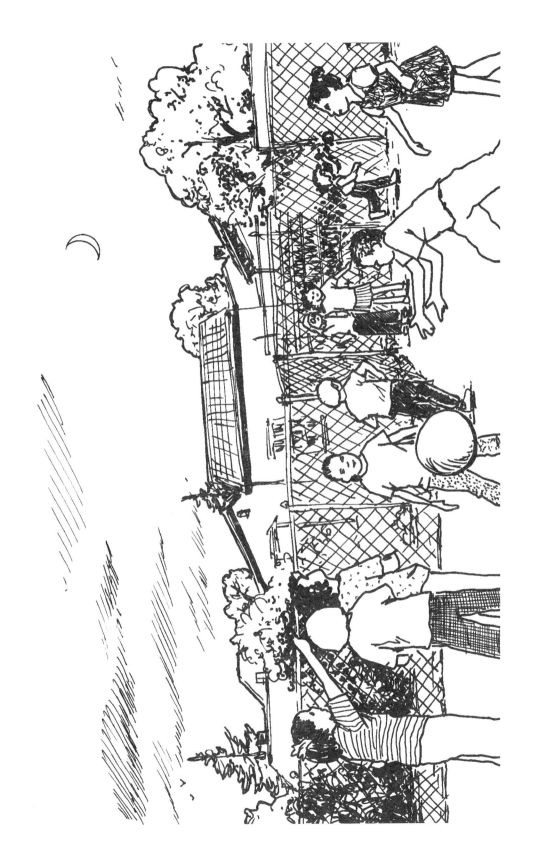

Look at the moon today.
Does it seem to fade away?

Does it seem to be a sliver,
seen both night and day?

Look at the moon again.
Is it absent from the sky?

If we wait a few more days, will it rise again so high?

Look at the moon each day and watch its pattern unfold. It helps us learn about our world. Each month its story told.

Paper - A Pressing Issue

Topic
Making paper from used paper

Key Question
How can we make our own paper?

Focus
Students will recycle paper to make paper.

Guiding Documents
Project 2061 Benchmarks
- *Things can be done to materials to change some of their properties, but not all materials respond the same way to what is done to them.*
- *Many materials can be recycled and used again, sometimes in different forms.*
- *Some kinds of materials are better than others for making any particular thing. Materials that are better in some ways (such as stronger or cheaper) may be worse in other ways (heavier or harder to cut).*
- *Several steps are usually involved in making things.*

NRC Standard
- *The supply of many resources are limited. If used, resources can be extended through recycling and decreased use.*

NCTM Standards
- *Develop the process of measuring and concepts related to units of measurement*
- *Make and use measurements in problems and everyday situations*

Math
Measurement

Science
Environmental science
   recycling

Integrated Processes
Observing
Comparing and contrasting
Recording
Generalizing

Materials
For the class:
   one or two blenders and/or hand mixers
   variety of used paper:
      notebook paper
      copy paper
      newspaper
      wrapping paper
      magazine paper
      envelopes
      computer paper
   warm water
   a tub to soak paper in for each kind of paper used
   measuring cups

For each group:
   wire mesh rectangle, 7" x 9"
   1 sandwich-size plastic bag
   1 newspaper
   hand lens or microscope
   1 piece of wood, 5" x 7" x 1/2"

Background Information
   If you use a hand lens or microscope to look closely at different types of paper, you will see hundreds of tiny fibers. These fibers are bonded together to make a thin, flat sheet of paper.
   Paper gets its name from the papyrus plant. Ancient Egyptians cut the papyrus into thin strips, criss-crossed them over each other, and pressed them to form sheets.
   Today paper is made from many things, but most often from wood that has been cut into chips and "cooked" to make tiny fibers, each less than 1/4" long. Other materials used in paper making include: cotton and linen rags which have fine fibers that are made into high-quality paper used for legal documents and money; hemp and manila hemp which have coarse fibers that are used to make strong wrapping paper and envelopes.

Management
1. Because of the mess this activity creates, you may want to make the pulp outdoors. To do this, you may need to find extension cords to provide electricity for running the blenders or hand mixers. Remind students that even though the mess is outdoors, they still need to clean the area.
2. DO NOT pour any left over pulp down the sink as this may clog the plumbing! Throw excess pulp away in the trash dumpsters.
3. To add color to your white paper, you can use a small bit of colored construction paper.
4. Use newspaper for the first part of the activity. Newspaper will produce a very gray recycled paper. For the second part, recycle old envelopes, notebook paper, etc.
5. This activity can easily take 25-30 minutes per group of students. It is suggested that you allow

one or two groups a day to go through a paper-making center or enlist the aid of another teacher or parent helper.

6. Part of the joy of discovery comes in *Part 2* of this activity. Allow students to be creative with the types of paper they use.

Procedure

Part 1

1. Have the students brainstorm the different ways they use paper in their daily life. Record their ideas on chart paper.

2. Distribute hand lenses and direct students to look at pieces of different types of paper. Ask them to describe the paper samples. How do they look the same? How are they different?

3. Ask students where they think paper comes from and instruct them to describe how they think paper might be made.

4. If available, read *Paper* by Andrew Langley (see *Curriculum Correlation*). Discuss the history, uses of paper, and the process of paper making with the students.

5. Talk about recycling paper. Tell the students that they are going to make paper from old newspapers. Take them through the steps of the process.

6. Instruct students to take the 7" x 9" wire mesh and bend up the four sides around the piece of wood. This will make their paper frame.

Figure 1

7. Give each student a couple pieces of newspaper and a plastic bag. Have them fold the paper to the same size as the inside of the plastic bag. Direct them to place this folded newspaper inside the bag.

Figure 2

Making the paper

1. Tear newspaper into 1" square pieces and place in a blender or bowl. Each student will need approximately one cup of paper.

2. Add about two cups warm water to each cup of torn paper and blend on high speed until you can't see any bits of paper. If needed, add more water to keep the mixture very watery.

3. If you want to make thin sheets of paper, pour the pulp into a tub half filled with water. For thicker paper, blend some more pulp and add it to the tub. The students will need to experiment to get the thickness they want.

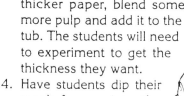

4. Have students dip their mesh frames into the pulp mixture and pull the frame straight up out of the water.

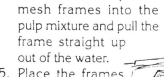

5. Place the frames with pulp on top of several layers of newspapers.

6. Using their prepared plastic bags with the folded newspaper inside, instruct the students to press down on top of the paper pulp to squeeze out the excess water. Repeat this several times until the water stops leaking out of the wire mesh.

7. Place the wire mesh with the pressed pulp outside to dry. Depending on the weather, in about 20-30 minutes, you should be able to turn over the mesh frame and tap on the back to release the paper. Place the paper on a flat surface to continue drying. Ironing the paper at a low setting while it is still moist will produce a smoother surface. If you leave the paper in the wire mesh to dry overnight, you will need to gently peel the paper out of the frame.

8. Once the paper is completely dry, allow students to view it with the hand lenses. Have them compare and contrast their recycled paper with the original paper they used.

Part 2

1. Allow students to choose a different type of used paper to use in making their next sample of recycled paper.

2. Take them through the process of making paper with each of the types of paper they wish to try.

3. Instruct the students to use a scientific method for preparing their experiments.

An example of a scientific method:

Questioning

What if... (statement or question from the student)
OR
I want to find out if...

Researching

Students should research library books, recall information gained from previous classroom experiences, or interview people involved in the field of whatever they are testing.

Predicting

"If (I do this)... then (this will happen) ..." statement by the student about what he/she thinks about the experiment based on the background information that has been gathered.

Investigating

Each student should write a "recipe" describing the entire experiment. It should include a step-by-step description of the procedure, the materials needed, a record of the results, a record of observations, and a conclusion based on the noted results. If the activity calls for a comparison, a chart could be designed to show those comparisons.

Further Investigating

The students should include some questions or wonderings about things they still want to find out about because of their experience with this investigation.

Discussion

1. Describe how the paper looks with the hand lens. What do you see through the hand lens that you cannot see by just looking at your paper?
2. Explain the steps you used to make your paper.
3. What do you notice about the differences between the paper you made and the paper you started out with?
4. What do you think you could do to make changes in the paper you make?
5. What do you think would happen if you used other types of paper?

Extensions

1. To show the recycling of a book, start with an old, discarded book, make it into pulp, make the paper, and then have the students write a new story on the paper and bind these pages into another book!
2. Use something other than paper to make the paper pulp; onion skins, straw, rags, etc.
3. Visit a paper mill or a print shop.
4. Visit a recycling station and learn about what other products are made from recycled paper.

Curriculum Correlation

Literature:

Langley, Andrew. *Paper.* Thomson Learning. New York. 1991.

Cherry, Lynne. *A River Ran Wild.* Gulliver Green/ Harcourt Brace Jovanovich. New York. 1992.

Home Link

1. Show the students the recycled logo. Instruct them to gather samples of items from home that were made from recycled paper.
2. Encourage students to join in a community or school project to recycle their newspapers.

A Sign of the Times

Topic
Products made from recycled paper

Key Question
What types of products or packages are made from recycled paper?

Focus
Students will become aware of different manufacturers that use recycled paper in their production.

Guiding Documents
Project 2061 Benchmarks
- *Many materials can be recycled and used again, sometimes in different forms.*
- *Some kinds of materials are better than others for making any particular thing. Materials that are better in some ways (such as stronger or cheaper) may be worse in other ways (heavier or harder to cut).*
- *Some materials can be used over again.*
- *Simple graphs can help to tell about observations.*

NRC Standard
- *The supply of many resources are limited. If used, resources can be extended through recycling and decreased use.*

NCTM Standards
- *Use mathematics in other curriculum areas*
- *Collect, organize and describe data*
- *Construct, read and interpret displays of data*
- *Formulate and solve problems that involve collecting and analyzing data*

Math
Graphing
Counting
Whole number operations

Science
Environmental science
   recycling

Integrated Processes
Observing
Sorting and classifying
Collecting and recording data
Interpreting data
Generalizing

Materials
For the class:
   large floor graph

Background Information
There is paper everywhere. We read newspapers and books made of paper. We write and draw on paper. Food comes wrapped or packed in paper. We have paper tissues, paper towels, paper labels, paper stamps, and even paper money. Our computers print out information on paper and our automobiles use paper in filters to keep the oil and air clean. Paper is also used in fireworks, the wrapping of gifts, and even in the hulls of boats. How much of this paper is made from recycled paper?

This activity is designed to help students be aware of manufacturers that use recycled paper in their production. The students will gather samples of items that are labeled as being made from recycled paper. They will sort, classify, graph, and compare the types of products they gather. The students will write letters of appreciation to the companies that manufacture products utilizing recycled paper and inquire as to the cost differences in using the recycled paper as compared to using virgin paper.

The students will look for similar products being marketed which are not made from or packaged in recycled paper products. They will then write to these manufacturers asking why they are not using recycled paper.

Management
1. Allow students at least one week to search for a variety of products made from recycled paper. (Ask students to bring in empty, clean packages of these items to avoid attracting unwanted pests and for safety reasons.) For items too large to bring into the classroom, ask students to try to draw pictures of the item or possibly photograph them.
2. Prepare a large area on the floor for the students to sort the items collected.
3. Before beginning the activity, make a large class graph that will accommodate the items collected.
4. Encourage the students to bring in packages that are completely intact so that the name of the product, the manufacturer, and address can be located. This will also allow you to double check for evidence of recycled paper being used.

Procedure

Part 1

1. Have your students brainstorm different things made from paper. Ask them for suggestions of items they think would be just as good made from recycled paper as they are made from virgin paper. Record their responses on chart paper.

2. Introduce the recycle symbol (*Figure 1*) and ask the students to look at home, in stores, etc. for items that have this symbol on them, stating that either the product or the packaging has been made from recycled paper. Some examples of containers which are made from recycled paper are: microwave popcorn, toothpaste, various crackers, cake mixes, cereals, pain relievers, quick rice products, cookies, plastic bags, and laundry soap.

Figure 1

3. Allow the students to collect these items for one week, bringing in samples or pictures.

4. As they bring new items in, let them sort and classify the collection. Ask the students to define their sorting categories. For example: packaging materials for food products, stationery or office supplies, magazines or books, etc. Keep a chart of these categories adding new categories as needed.

5. After a week of collecting, lead the students in a discussion to decide on appropriate labels for a class graph to represent the products collected. Label the graph and glue or tape samples to it.

6. Discuss the graph with the students and lead them in a discussion as to the types of products that seem to be represented more than others. Compare the results with the original chart the students made of the items they thought could be made from recycled paper.

Part 2

1. Take a closer look at the products collected. Make a list of all the manufacturers of these products. Use a tally mark beside each company's name to indicate a product using recycled materials. Discuss the chart.

2. Direct students to write letters (individually or as a class) to these companies in appreciation for their efforts to use recycled paper. In the letters, have the students inquire as to whether or not it is more expensive to use recycled paper as opposed to virgin paper. Direct them to ask for a possible cost comparison. If the cost is higher, the company will probably offer their rationale as to the added cost of the use of recycled paper.

Part 3

1. Ask students to now find similar products from companies who are not using recycled paper.

2. After the students have collected for one week, chart the results according to the company and products.

3. Direct the students to write letters to these companies stating that there was no indication of the use of recycled paper in the manufacturing of the product or packaging. Inquire if they use recycled paper in their packaging. Your students might want to suggest that they consider changing their use of virgin paper to the use of recycled paper in the manufacturing of their product or in the packaging of their product. Direct the students to describe the investigation in which they have been involved and to cite information from their charts and graphs.

4. Wait for responses from the various companies and compare them.

Discussion

1. For what type of products did the class gather the most evidence of recycling?

2. Look at the list of products you thought might be made from recycled paper. How many of these items were collected? Were any not found? Why do you think this happened? What items did you find that you didn't think of the first time we brainstormed suggestions?

3. Which companies seem to use recycled paper more than other companies? Why do you think these companies have made the decision to use recycled paper?

4. For the products or packages not made from recycled paper, why do you think these companies have decided not to use recycled paper?

5. Do the products or packages made with recycled paper look different from those of virgin paper? Explain.

6. Does it make a difference to you if the products you buy are wrapped in recycled paper or virgin paper? Why?

7. Explain why it is beneficial to use recycled paper.
8. Explain the negative aspects for companies who are using recycled paper.
9. If you were the president of a company, explain why you would or would not use recycled paper products.
10. What are some things you can do to encourage companies to use recycled paper?

Extensions
1. Conduct a consumer awareness survey with the products gathered. Compare the cost of products made with recycled paper and those that are not. Is there a correlation between the use of recycled paper and cost of the product?
2. Visit a recycling station and learn about the process involved in recycling paper.
3. Write letters to various businesses in your area asking them what products they are using that are made from recycled materials.
4. Allow students to organize a campaign to encourage people of their community to purchase products made of or packaged with recycled paper.
5. Ask students to research different ways recycling paper impacts their community. Be sure to encourage them to find the negative aspects as well as the beneficial implications.

Words by Suzy Gazlay

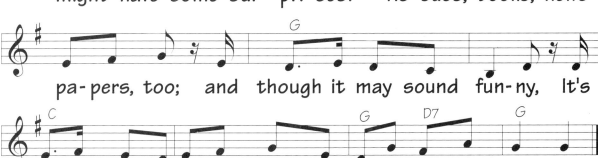

We use it when we paint or draw;
To write a note or letter;
For pictures, photos, posters too
To make our homes look better;
Cardboard boxes, paper towels;
For making things quite clever;
Computers print on paper, too —
The list could go forever!

If no more paper could be made,
Would we be glad? I doubt it!
There's so much paper in our lives
We'd find it hard without it.
But paper's mostly made from trees
That take a long time growing.
There has to be a better way —
Some progress we are showing!

New paper can be made from old
While resources reclaiming.
We'll leave the trees for other things —
For wise use we are aiming.
Recycling makes a lot of sense:
It saves the trees while using
The paper trash we'd throw away —
Recycling we are choosing!

After Lunch

Topic
Decomposition

Key Question
What will happen to our lunch garbage if we bury it for a couple of months?

Focus
Students will make a garbage "time capsule" and bury it in the ground. Two months later, they will evaluate its contents.

Guiding Documents
Project 2061 Benchmark
- *Change is something that happens to many things.*

NRC Standard
- *All organisms cause changes in the environment where they live. Some of these changes are detrimental to the organism or other organisms, whereas others are beneficial.*

NCTM Standard
- *Construct, read and interpret displays of data*

Math
Charting

Science
Life science
    decomposition
Ecology

Integrated Processes
Observing
Comparing and contrasting
Predicting
Generalizing

Materials
For the class:
    nylon stocking
    rubber band
    shovel
    garbage consisting of items from students' lunches:
        drink containers (plastic or glass), food containers, plastic forks or spoons, aluminum foil, plastic bags, wax paper, plastic wrap, leftover food
    chart paper
    plastic gloves

Background Information
A landfill is a site where garbage is dumped. A natural pit is often selected and is deepened by earth-moving machines. A covering is usually used to line the pit to keep toxins from the garbage out of the ground water. Garbage is then layered in the pit. Each layer is covered with dirt.

Eighty percent of our garbage is put in landfills. Ten percent is burned and the other ten percent is recycled. If we produce less garbage by recycling, reusing, and refusing, we can greatly reduce the rate at which we are adding to our landfills.

Management
1. Find a site where the time capsule can be buried. Make a marker so you can find the site when you want to unearth the capsule. A decomposition chamber can be made in an old trash can which is filled with dirt. While not as effective, it works if no other place is available.
2. Make sure students are involved in both the burying procedure and the unearthing procedure.
3. Ask the custodian to save several bags of lunch garbage for the class to select contents.
4. The capsule is a single nylon stocking, or a leg cut from a pair of panty hose.
5. As you make the capsule, place the garbage in the hose so that it is layered loosely and will be exposed to the soil surrounding it.
6. The capsule should be buried for a minimum of two months.
7. Prepare a chart with *Before* and *After* columns.

Procedure
Planning and predicting about the time capsule.
1. Discuss where the garbage from lunch goes.
2. Have students draw a picture or discuss what they think the garbage can looks like after lunch. Collect their predictions.
3. Take the class outdoors, perhaps to the school dumpster. Use an old newspaper on which to spread out the contents of the bag of lunch garbage the custodian has saved. Discuss the contents and have the students select items for the time capsule. Any student that touches the contents should wear plastic gloves.
5. Make a list of the contents.
6. Layer the contents in the hose so that they have the greatest amount of exposure to the soil.

7. Close the top of the hose with a rubber band. Carry it to the burial site making certain the elements don't get compressed together.

8. At the site dig a deep, narrow hole. It may be necessary for an adult to start the hole, but if possible, let the students take turns digging. Mark the site.

9. Upon returning to the classroom, have students use the list to illustrate the time capsule's components on sticky notes. Direct the students to place the sticky notes on the chart in the *Before* column.

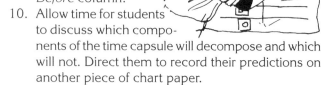

10. Allow time for students to discuss which components of the time capsule will decompose and which will not. Direct them to record their predictions on another piece of chart paper.

Unearthing the Time Capsule

11. Have students unearth the capsule after about two months.

12. Put on plastic gloves and dump the contents of the capsule on a sheet of newspaper. Use a stick to spread out the contents.

13. Have several students draw a picture of the changes in each buried item and put them in the last column on the chart labeled *After*. As a class, go back and compare the predictions with the results.

14. After discussing each item, read the suggested literature relating to landfills. Ask the students what they could change when packing a lunch if they wanted to reduce the amount of material going into the landfill. Give each student the activity sheet and have them design an Earth-friendly lunch.

Discussion

1. How can we reduce the amount of garbage we make at lunch?
2. What can you do at home to make less garbage?
3. What does decompose mean? Which items decomposed? Which items didn't?
4. Why do we want our garbage to decompose?

Extensions

1. Make a compost pile for observation.
2. Have parents help make cloth lunch bags for the class and use them.

3. Find out where your garbage goes. Visit a local landfill.
4. Reduce, reuse, recycle, and refuse!

Curriculum Correlation
Literature
   Robinson, Fay. *Too Much Trash*. Children's Press. Chicago. 1995.

Design an Earth-friendly lunch.

A New Look for an Old Bag

Topic
Reuse

Key Question
How can we use a paper bag again?

Focus
Students will learn how to reuse a paper bag to construct a container.

Guiding Documents
Project 2061 Benchmark
- *Some materials can be used over and over again.*

NRC Standard
- *The supply of many resources is limited. If used, resources can be extended through recycling and decreased use.*

NCTM Standards
- *Recognize and appreciate geometry in their world*
- *Develop spatial sense*

Math
Measuring
Counting

Science
Environmental science
    solid waste management

Integrated Processes
Observing
Communicating
Comparing and contrasting

Materials
For each student:
    3 used grocery bags, same size

Optional for the class:
    assorted collection of used bows, streamers,
        construction paper and stickers
    hole punch

Background Information
Each year Americans throw away some 400 million pounds of garbage. The United States has only 5% of the world's population but produces 30% of the world's garbage. When we throw away something, it does not just "go away" — most of it goes into the garbage. This garbage is in turn taken to a sanitary landfill.

Landfills pose many problems. One problem is that landfills take up a lot of land that could be used for other purposes. Another problem is the toxic liquid that can be created when water percolates through the garbage in our landfills. In addition to our problems with disposing of solid waste, we are also using up natural resources which are limited in supply.

Our choices in helping to alleviate these issues are recycling, reducing, reusing, and refusing. Reducing and refusing to use materials are viable options. However, for young learners, these options are not always in their control. Recycling and reusing are options that are quite do-able for them and they are capable of sharing these efforts with other members of their families. Simple things like using a paper bag more than once are things that children can do. This activity builds on this idea and hopefully launches learners into thinking about reuse as well as recycling.

Management
1. For young learners it is recommended that you do this in groups of six or less.
2. Provide extra paper bags in case some tear in the construction process.

Procedure
1. Hold up a paper bag and ask the students what their family does with used grocery bags. As students are sharing how they have seen old grocery bags used at home, record their thoughts in two unlabeled columns on the chalkboard. For example, a student might suggest that the family uses the old bags to hold trash. Record that in a column. They might describe how they put bags in the recycling stack with the old newspapers. Record this in another column. As you continue recording, place all *recycling* ideas in one column and *reusing* in another. Ask the students why they think you put their ideas in two columns. With younger students you may want to read what you placed in each column.
2. Tell students that today they are going to be reusing old paper bags in a different way.
3. Hold up the bag and show them how to roll the bag down about two finger widths creating a

downward cuff. (See illustration)

4. After the first cuff has been established show them how to keep rolling until the bag is rolled to its base.

5. Hold up a second bag and tell them they are going to be rolling that bag down but not quite as far. Show them how to keep rolling and where to stop. This bag should fit snugly in the first rolled bag so the last roll falls right above the roll of the first bag. (See illustration)

6. Once the double bag construction has been completed, use a third bag to show the students how to roll the top down three or four rolls. (Two students can actually use one bag.)

7. Cut this roll off to form a loop that will become a handle.

8. After forming the handle, show students how to slip it around the basket structure until it is positioned in the middle of the bag. (See illustration.) Using a hole punch, create a hole on either side of the handle and then slip a piece of old ribbon in one side of the hole and out the other. Tie the ribbon to secure the handle in place.

9. Invite students to decorate their bag with old wrapping paper, streamers, or old greeting cards. Discuss the fact that all the materials have been used before.

10. Inform the students that they can use their baskets to store their work materials like scissors, pencils, markers, etc.

11. Bring students together in a discussion group and ask them if they can think of other items that can be reused. Add their suggestions to the original list.

12. Read the book *Recycle* (see *Curriculum Correlation*) and emphasize how important it is to reuse items.

Discussion

1. Explain in your own words what it means to reuse something.

2. What items did we reuse to make our baskets? What are some other items that can be reused?

3. Why is it just as important to reuse and to recycle things?

4. Can you invent a way to use something again? Give an example.

5. What would you say to someone who was throwing a used paper bag away?

Extensions

1. Use old smaller lunch bags as decorative planters by making them and then lining them with used plastic grocery bags.

2. Challenge students to use a paper bag over and over again. Have them keep a tally on the outside of the bag to record the number of times they have used the bag. The bags could be used in a real graph format in which students graph by number of times used.

Curriculum Correlation

Literature:

Gibbons, Gail. *Recycle*. Little, Brown and Co. Boston. 1992.

Wilcox, Charlotte. *Trash*. Carolrhoda Books. Minneapolis. 1988.

Home Link

Let the students take the paper bag basket home and share what they learned about reuse with their parents.

Bibliography

Allen, Marjorie. and N. Rotner. *Changes*. Macmillan Publishing Co. New York. 1991.

Cherry, Lynne. *A River Ran Wild*. Gulliver Green/Harcourt Brace Jovanovich. New York. 1992.

Fowler, Allan. *The Sun Is Always Shining Somewhere*. Children's Press. Chicago. 1991.

Gibbons Gail. *Monarch Butterfly*. Holiday House. New York. 1989.

Gibbons, Gail. *Sun Up, Sun Down*. Harcourt Brace Jovanovich. San Diego. 1983.

Gibbons, Gail. *The Seasons of Arnold's Apple Tree*. Harcourt Brace Jovanovich. New York. 1984.

Griffin, Sandra Ure. *Earth Cycles*. Walker and Co. New York.1989.

Ichikawa, Satomi. *Happy Birthday: A Book of Birthday Celebrations*. Philomel Books. New York. 1987.

Johnston. Tony. *Yonder*. Dial Books. New York. 1988.

King, Elizabeth. *The Pumpkin Patch*. Dutton Children's Book. New York. 1990.

Kroll, Steven. *It's Groundhog Day*. Scholastic, Inc. New York. 1987.

Langley, Andrew. *Paper*. Thomson Learning. New York. 1991

Lavies, Bianca. *Compost Critter*. Dutton Children's Books. New York. 1993.

Markle, Sandra. *Outside and Inside Trees*. Bradbury Press. New York. 1993.

Marzollo, Jean. *Sun Song*. HarperCollins Publishers. New York. 1995.

Ray, Mary Lyn. *Pumkins*. Harcourt Brace Jovanovich. San Diego. 1992

Robinson, Faye. *Too Much Trash*. Children's Press. Chicago. 1985.

Rosenfeld, Christel. *Sunflower*. Roberts Rinehart Publishers. Niwot, CO. 1991.

Ross, Michael Elsohn. *Cycles, Cycles, Cycles*. Yosemite Association. 1979.

Ryder, Joanne. *Where Butterflies Grow*. Lodestar Books, Dutton Publishing. New York. 1989.

Titherington, Jeanne. *Pumpkin, Pumpkin*. Scholastic, Inc. New York. 1986.

Tompert, Ann. *Nothing Sticks Like A Shadow*. Houghton Mifflin Co. Boston. 1984.

Tresselt, Alvin. *The Gift of the Tree*. Lorthrop, Lee and Shepard Books. New York. 1992.

Whalley, Paul. *Butterfly and Moth: An Eyewitness Book*. Alfred A. Knopf. New York. 1988.

Willard, Nancy. *Nightgown of the Sullen Moon*. Harcourt Brace Jovanovich. Orlando, FL. 1983.

Zolotow, Charlotte. *Over and Over*. Harper and Row. New York. 1957.

Zolotow, Charlotte. *When the Wind Stops*. HarperCollins Publishers. New York. 1992.

The AIMS Program

AIMS is the acronym for "Activities Integrating Mathematics and Science." Such integration enriches learning and makes it meaningful and holistic. AIMS began as a project of Fresno Pacific University to integrate the study of mathematics and science in grades K-9, but has since expanded to include language arts, social studies, and other disciplines.

AIMS is a continuing program of the non-profit AIMS Education Foundation. It had its inception in a National Science Foundation funded program whose purpose was to explore the effectiveness of integrating mathematics and science. The project directors in cooperation with 80 elementary classroom teachers devoted two years to a thorough field-testing of the results and implications of integration.

The approach met with such positive results that the decision was made to launch a program to create instructional materials incorporating this concept. Despite the fact that thoughtful educators have long recommended an integrative approach, very little appropriate material was available in 1981 when the project began. A series of writing projects have ensued and today the AIMS Education Foundation is committed to continue the creation of new integrated activities on a permanent basis.

The AIMS program is funded through the sale of this developing series of books and proceeds from the Foundation's endowment. All net income from program and products flows into a trust fund administered by the AIMS Education Foundation. Use of these funds is restricted to support of research, development, and publication of new materials. Writers donate all their rights to the Foundation to support its on-going program. No royalties are paid to the writers.

The rationale for integration lies in the fact that science, mathematics, language arts, social studies, etc., are integrally interwoven in the real world from which it follows that they should be similarly treated in the classroom where we are preparing students to live in that world. Teachers who use the AIMS program give enthusiastic endorsement to the effectiveness of this approach.

Science encompasses the art of questioning, investigating, hypothesizing, discovering, and communicating. Mathematics is the language that provides clarity, objectivity, and understanding. The language arts provide us powerful tools of communication. Many of the major contemporary societal issues stem from advancements in science and must be studied in the context of the social sciences. Therefore, it is timely that all of us take seriously a more holistic mode of educating our students. This goal motivates all who are associated with the AIMS Program. We invite you to join us in this effort.

Meaningful integration of knowledge is a major recommendation coming from the nation's professional science and mathematics associations. The American Association for the Advancement of Science in *Science for All Americans* strongly recommends the integration of mathematics, science, and technology. The National Council of Teachers of Mathematics places strong emphasis on applications of mathematics such as are found in science investigations. AIMS is fully aligned with these recommendations.

Extensive field testing of AIMS investigations confirms these beneficial results.

1. Mathematics becomes more meaningful, hence more useful, when it is applied to situations that interest students.
2. The extent to which science is studied and understood is increased, with a significant economy of time, when mathematics and science are integrated.
3. There is improved quality of learning and retention, supporting the thesis that learning which is meaningful and relevant is more effective.
4. Motivation and involvement are increased dramatically as students investigate real-world situations and participate actively in the process.

We invite you to become part of this classroom teacher movement by using an integrated approach to learning and sharing any suggestions you may have. The AIMS Program welcomes you!

AIMS Education Foundation Programs

A Day with AIMS

Intensive one-day workshops are offered to introduce educators to the philosophy and rationale of AIMS. Participants will discuss the methodology of AIMS and the strategies by which AIMS principles may be incorporated into curriculum. Each participant will take part in a variety of hands-on AIMS investigations to gain an understanding of such aspects as the scientific/mathematical content, classroom management, and connections with other curricular areas. *A Day with AIMS* workshops may be offered anywhere in the United States. Necessary supplies and take-home materials are usually included in the enrollment fee.

A Week with AIMS

Throughout the nation, AIMS offers many one-week workshops each year, usually in the summer. Each workshop lasts five days and includes at least 30 hours of AIMS hands-on instruction. Participants are grouped according to the grade level(s) in which they are interested. Instructors are members of the AIMS Instructional Leadership Network. Supplies for the activities and a generous supply of take-home materials are included in the enrollment fee. Sites are selected on the basis of applications submitted by educational organizations. If chosen to host a workshop, the host agency agrees to provide specified facilities and cooperate in the promotion of the workshop. The AIMS Education Foundation supplies workshop materials as well as the travel, housing, and meals for instructors.

AIMS One-Week Perspectives Workshops

Each summer, Fresno Pacific University offers AIMS one-week workshops on its campus in Fresno, California. AIMS Program Directors and highly qualified members of the AIMS National Leadership Network serve as instructors.

The Science Festival and the Festival of Mathematics

Each summer, Fresno Pacific University offers a Science Festival and a Festival of Mathematics. These festivals have gained national recognition as inspiring and challenging experiences, giving unique opportunities to experience hands-on mathematics and science in topical and grade-level groups. Guest faculty includes some of the nation's most highly regarded mathematics and science educators. Supplies and take-home materials are included in the enrollment fee.

The AIMS Instructional Leadership Program

This is an AIMS staff-development program seeking to prepare facilitators for leadership roles in science/math education in their home districts or regions. Upon successful completion of the program, trained facilitators become members of the AIMS Instructional Leadership Network, qualified to conduct AIMS workshops, teach AIMS in-service courses for college credit, and serve as AIMS consultants. Intensive training is provided in mathematics, science, process and thinking skills, workshop management, and other relevant topics.

College Credit and Grants

Those who participate in workshops may often qualify for college credit. If the workshop takes place on the campus of Fresno Pacific University, that institution may grant appropriate credit. If the workshop takes place off-campus, arrangements can sometimes be made for credit to be granted by another college or university. In addition, the applicant's home school district is often willing to grant in-service or professional development credit. Many educators who participate in AIMS workshops are recipients of various types of educational grants, either local or national. Nationally known foundations and funding agencies have long recognized the value of AIMS mathematics and science workshops to educators. The AIMS Education Foundation encourages educators interested in attending or hosting workshops to explore the possibilities suggested above. Although the Foundation strongly supports such interest, it reminds applicants that they have the primary responsibility for fulfilling *current* requirements.

For current information regarding the programs described above, please complete the following:

Information Request

Please send current information on the items checked:

___ *Basic Information Packet* on AIMS materials	___ *AIMS One-Week Perspectives* workshops
___ *Festival of Mathematics*	___ *A Week with AIMS* workshops
___ *Science Festival*	___ Hosting information for *A Day with AIMS* workshops
___ *AIMS Instructional Leadership Program*	___ Hosting information for *A Week with AIMS* workshops

Name _____ Phone _____

Address _____
       Street   City   State   Zip

AIMS Program Publications

GRADES K-4 SERIES

Bats Incredible
Brinca de Alegria Hacia la Primavera con las Matemáticas y Ciencias
Cáete de Gusto Hacia el Otoño con la Matemática y Ciencias
Cycles of Knowing and Growing
Fall Into Math and Science
Field Detectives
Glide Into Winter With Math and Science
Hardhatting in a Geo-World (Revised Edition, 1996)
Jaw Breakers and Heart Thumpers (Revised Edition, 1995)
Los Cincos Sentidos
Overhead and Underfoot (Revised Edition, 1994)
Patine al Invierno con Matemáticas y Ciencias
Popping With Power (Revised Edition, 1996)
Primariamente Física (Revised Edition, 1994)
Primarily Earth
Primariamente Plantas
Primarily Physics (Revised Edition, 1994)
Primarily Plants
Sense-able Science
Spring Into Math and Science
Under Construction

GRADES K-6 SERIES

Budding Botanist
Critters
El Botanista Principiante
Mostly Magnets
Ositos Nada Más
Primarily Bears
Principalmente Imanes
Water Precious Water

GRADES 5-9 SERIES

Actions with Fractions
Brick Layers
Conexiones Eléctricas
Down to Earth
Electrical Connections
Finding Your Bearings (Revised Edition, 1996)
Floaters and Sinkers (Revised Edition, 1995)
From Head to Toe
Fun With Foods
Historical Connections in Mathematics, Volume I
Historical Connections in Mathematics, Volume II
Historical Connections in Mathematics, Volume III
Machine Shop
Magnificent Microworld Adventures
Math + Science, A Solution
Off the Wall Science: A Poster Series Revisited
Our Wonderful World
Out of This World (Revised Edition, 1994)
Pieces and Patterns, A Patchwork in Math and Science
Piezas y Diseños, un Mosaic de Matemáticas y Ciencias
Soap Films and Bubbles
Spatial Visualization
The Sky's the Limit (Revised Edition, 1994)
The Amazing Circle, Volume 1
Through the Eyes of the Explorers:
    Minds-on Math & Mapping
What's Next, Volume 1
What's Next, Volume 2
What's Next, Volume 3

For further information write to:

AIMS Education Foundation • P.O. Box 8120 • Fresno, California 93747-8120

We invite you to subscribe to $\mathcal{AIMS}$!

Each issue of $\mathcal{AIMS}$ contains a variety of material useful to educators at all grade levels. Feature articles of lasting value deal with topics such as mathematical or science concepts, curriculum, assessment, the teaching of process skills, and historical background. Several of the latest AIMS math/science investigations are always included, along with their reproducible activity sheets. As needs direct and space allows, various issues contain news of current developments, such as workshop schedules, activities of the AIMS Instructional Leadership Network, and announcements of upcoming publications.

$\mathcal{AIMS}$ is published monthly, August through May. Subscriptions are on an annual basis only. A subscription entered at any time will begin with the next issue, but will also include the previous issues of that volume. Readers have preferred this arrangement because articles and activities within an annual volume are often interrelated.

Please note that an $\mathcal{AIMS}$ subscription automatically includes duplication rights for one school site for all issues included in the subscription. Many schools build cost-effective library resources with their subscriptions.

YES! I am interested in subscribing to $\mathcal{AIMS}$.

Name _____   Home Phone _____

Address _____   City, State, Zip _____

Please send the following volumes (subject to availability):

_____ Volume IV   (1989-90) $30.00   _____ Volume IX   (1994-95) $30.00

_____ Volume V   (1990-91) $30.00   _____ Volume X   (1995-96) $30.00

_____ Volume VI   (1991-92) $30.00   _____ Volume XI   (1996-97) $30.00

_____ Volume VII   (1992-93) $30.00   _____ Volume XII   (1997-98) $30.00

_____ **Limited offer: Volumes XII & XIII (1997-99) $55.00**
(Note: Prices may change without notice)

Check your method of payment:

❏ Check enclosed in the amount of $ _____

❏ Purchase order attached (Please include the P.O.#, the authorizing signature, and position of the authorizing person.)

❏ Credit Card   ❏ Visa   ❏ MasterCard   Amount $ _____

Card # _____   Expiration Date _____

Signature _____   Today's Date _____

Make checks payable to **AIMS Education Foundation**.
Mail to $\mathcal{AIMS}$ magazine, P.O. Box 8120, Fresno, CA 93747-8120.
Phone (209) 255-4094 or (888) 733-2467   FAX (209) 255-6396
AIMS Homepage: http://www.AIMSedu.org/

AIMS Duplication Rights Program

AIMS has received many requests from school districts for the purchase of unlimited duplication rights to AIMS materials. In response, the AIMS Education Foundation has formulated the program outlined below. There is a built-in flexibility which, we trust, will provide for those who use AIMS materials extensively to purchase such rights for either individual activities or entire books.

It is the goal of the AIMS Education Foundation to make its materials and programs available at reasonable cost. All income from the sale of publications and duplication rights is used to support AIMS programs; hence, strict adherence to regulations governing duplication is essential. Duplication of AIMS materials beyond limits set by copyright laws and those specified below is strictly forbidden.

Limited Duplication Rights

Any purchaser of an AIMS book may make up to *200 copies* of any activity in that book for use at *one school site*. Beyond that, rights must be purchased according to the appropriate category.

Unlimited Duplication Rights for Single Activities

An individual or school may purchase the right to make an unlimited number of copies of a single activity. The royalty is $5.00 per activity per school site.

Examples: 3 activities x 1 site x $5.00 = $15.00
9 activities x 3 sites x $5.00 = $135.00

Unlimited Duplication Rights for Entire Books

A school or district may purchase the right to make an unlimited number of copies of a single, *specified* book. The royalty is $20.00 per book per school site. This is in addition to the cost of the book.

Examples: 5 books x 1 site   x $20.00 = $100.00
12 books x 10 sites x $20.00 = $2400.00

Magazine/Newsletter Duplication Rights

Members of the AIMS Education Foundation who purchase the *AIMS* magazine/*Newsletter* are hereby granted permission to make up to 200 copies of any portion of it, provided these copies will be used for educational purposes.

Workshop Instructors' Duplication Rights

Workshop instructors may distribute to registered workshop participants a maximum of 100 copies of any article and/or 100 copies of no more than eight activities, provided these six conditions are met:

1. Since all AIMS activities are based upon the *AIMS Model of Mathematics* and the *AIMS Model of Learning*, leaders must include in their presentations an explanation of these two models.
2. Workshop instructors must relate the AIMS activities presented to these basic explanations of the AIMS philosophy of education.
3. The copyright notice must appear on all materials distributed.
4. Instructors must provide information enabling participants to apply for membership in the AIMS Education Foundation or order books from the Foundation.
5. Instructors must inform participants of their limited duplication rights as outlined below.
6. Only student pages may be duplicated.

Written permission must be obtained for duplication beyond the limits listed above. Additional royalty payments may be required.

Workshop Participants' Rights

Those enrolled in workshops in which AIMS student activity sheets are distributed may duplicate a maximum of 35 copies or enough to use the lessons one time with one class, whichever is less. Beyond that, rights must be purchased according to the appropriate category.

Application for Duplication Rights

The purchasing agency or individual must clearly specify the following:
1. Name, address, and telephone number
2. Titles of the books for Unlimited Duplication Rights contracts
3. Titles of activities for Unlimited Duplication Rights contracts
4. Names and addresses of school sites for which duplication rights are being purchased.

NOTE: Books to be duplicated must be purchased separately and are not included in the contract for Unlimited Duplication Rights.

The requested duplication rights are automatically authorized when proper payment is received, although a *Certificate of Duplication Rights* will be issued when the application is processed.

Address all correspondence to: **Contract Division**
AIMS Education Foundation
P.O. Box 8120
Fresno, CA 93747-8120